PSYCHODYNAMIC TENNIS

PSYCHODYNAMIC TENNIS

You, Your Opponent, and Other Obstacles to Perfection

by Ethan Gologor

William Morrow and Company, Inc.   New York   1979

Library of Congress Cataloging in Publication Data

Gologor, Ethan.
   Psychodynamic tennis.

   Includes index.
   1. Tennis—Psychological aspects. I. Title.
GV1002.9.P75G64   796.34′2′01   78-31247
ISBN 0-688-03466-7

PATTY LOWY   BOOK DESIGN

Printed in the United States of America.

First Edition

1   2   3   4   5   6   7   8   9   10

To Harry and Esther
and their 1923 Slazenger
with the 6¼" grip

Preface

THE PROBLEM

Five of the last ten people I met swore that no matter how the social pressure increases, no matter how much their colleagues or in-laws insist, they're steadfastly going to refuse to get out there, or they're not going to think about it if they do, or they're not going to take it seriously, or they're not going to talk about it incessantly. That's a lot of energy to spend on not doing something. And the other five were tennis fanatics and could talk only about tennis and other tennis fanatics.

I think something can be done for both groups. For my own reasons, I like playing tennis, but I also like people who refuse to, for their own reasons. I want people to play better tennis, more interesting tennis, more thoughtful tennis, because I think that makes the game more interesting, but I also would like those who don't-care-to-thank-you to be interested in their reasons. Some of those reasons may have to do with one's own bad experiences or "noncompetitive" personality, but most, I am convinced, are reactions against participating in the complexities of social behavior that tennis elicits. Like a few other things that have fallen into the hands of psychologists, tennis is not just tennis any longer.

Anyone who's been exposed to some tennis instruction, first- or secondhand, can recognize that imperfection does not result from ignorance of the proper form. Or when it does, removing the ignorance doesn't necessarily improve one's game. One wants to know not only how to correct one's toss to prevent double-faulting, but why one suddenly forgets how when he's at game point, for the first time, against a higher-ranked opponent. One wants to know why, after a prolonged exchange which seems testimony to the even caliber of the opponents, the winner moves on to an easy victory. One wants to know why, after Peter Fleming has been dominating a match against Raul Ramirez for three sets, he suddenly double-faults three times and loses service twice in a row. (See Chapter 6, if you think "choking" is all there is to it. Prior to Fleming's collapse, Ramirez had run around his backhand for the first time and *missed the shot*. But it was definitely the turning point.) To most of us, information about twisting the torso, snapping the wrist, and getting the racquet back seems beside the point. Like advice on how to meet people, secure a job, and take better charge of our own lives, the diagnosis of the ailment may be fine, but the therapy provided unhelpful. We don't need to know that we should prepare our racquets (or résumés, or conversational openers to the attractive stranger) well ahead of time, but why, knowing that we should, we still don't do it. The shortcoming, it appears, isn't just technical.

THE SOLUTION

With those readers who might be suspicious about using psychology to improve anything, I am deeply sympathetic. There is nothing like psychological training itself to make one wary about psychologists' ability to effect change, even once the mysteries have been unraveled. I can remember one instance in a seminar, after long hours spent analyzing a client's problems, finding parallels in other behavior patterns, and developing sensitive instruments to discern the nature of his destructive path, when the supervisor suggested that cure might begin with "bibliotherapy." I beg your pardon? Bibliotherapy. Give him certain books to read on the subject.

Certainly, the premise that books or ideas might cure was not what I found offensive, but to hear *psychology* announce that it had found a technique of therapy—Read Books—was a bit disquieting.[1] For hadn't it been psychology that had announced somewhere along the way that insight and cure would be reached not through the ideas we think are true, not through what we hear from others, not through the saga of human woes narrated by the sufferer, not through the mere search for fulfillment or release from pain, but through something beyond, something special within that mystery of the unconscious or sheltered motives or self-defeating impulses or simultaneously bizarre and familiar patterns of behavior that all of us display despite ourselves, and that are hidden from us, hidden for good psychological reasons, hidden in total or important part, hidden, kept hidden, and furnished with continual energy to remain hidden? For this revolutionary psychology to proclaim its technique for cure—Read Books—was tantamount to the acupuncture-trained Maharishi on the cancer ward of Sloan-Kettering, the one you'd been waiting to consult for three months, telling you, for a $5,000 fee, to eat a balanced diet and try to get plenty of exercise.

And yet, that's often just what you are told and just what you need to know. Bibliotherapy didn't cure my client,

[1] I am here talking of clinical psychology, the branch of the field most directly involved with therapy. If you've gotten lost in the therapy market recently, that's probably because it's begun to resemble a Baskin-Robbins emporium. This month's features include "activities" therapy (playing Scrabble?), "reality" therapy (Tell it like it is, baby?), natal therapy (A la recherche du temps perdu?), not to mention dance therapy, play therapy, art therapy, drama therapy (Express yourself, why don't you, in one way or another) before one discovers the somewhat congealed classical items in the back freezer and their numerous imitators.

but it certainly got him started. And it got me started on liking the idea. His reading sources, after all, were available much more often than his therapist. Indeed, it occurred to me that much of the ineffable expertise lurking in the "talent" or "experience" or "intuition" of the specialists might have served quite a different purpose than the interest of the client. It might have kept them continually needed. So I decided I liked my Maharishi who didn't disguise his advice with Latin diagnoses (to mix a metaphor). And I liked bibliotherapy. If he knows what he's doing, shouldn't the analyst be able to communicate his methods? And if the public still feels some resentment over the specialist's discovering the obvious, there is at least the consolation that it makes it much easier for all of us to become specialists.

ACKNOWLEDGMENTS

There may be some things left in the world that you can do alone, but playing tennis isn't one of them. I have been lucky enough to have engaged formidable partners, to each of whom I am grateful: Jerry Cantor, Marla Chaikin, Linda Epstein, Nancy Haberman, Anita Washam, Renee Weber, and Steven Zaretzky, for providing anything from the hidden location of important resources to forceful challenges to the manuscript; Louise Bernikow, for considerable help in getting the project started; Melvin Fishman, for his perspective, different enough from mine but generously consigned for the duration; Jim Landis, for a methodical, yet especially gentle hand.

My appreciation also goes to Gordon Anderson, Freddy Baez, Henry "Sam" Nagai, and Phil Winters for their spirited management, formal and informal, of my favorite public courts. And for the use of its typing and Frederick Lewis Allen Memorial Rooms, I am grateful to the New York Public Library.

For their characteristic tolerance, even while skeptical, of those mysterious disappearances to the courts to do "papa's work," I thank Matthew and Benjamin. And for continuing to do what she does so well, underediting and overestimating others' idiosyncratic visions, I am, as always, indebted to Masha.

Contents

14   ① PSYCHODYNAMIC TENNIS

Contents ◍ 15

CHAPTER 1

Sports and Shrinks

Of course, this marriage is nothing new. I may not have the right movie in mind, but I'm sure that before Kirk Douglas or Charlton Heston went off to do battle with the Black Knight of Moravia, he fell to one knee and prayed to Amenhotep IV, ruler of his courage, or asked for Rhonda Fleming's special sword-on-shoulder or hand-on-halo blessing. Not with deft saber alone does our hero distinguish himself, but—since it's the only item missing from the black-hooded foe's arsenal of weapons—through display of the specially dispensated moral righteousness, which carries him to victory.

A little more recently, pronouncements like the following have become commonplace in sports. George Allen, then coach of the Washington Redskins football team, was asked toward the end of the season what he thought were the chances for his team's making the playoffs, and he replied that at this point, you don't win with talent, you win with "character." Descriptions like a player's being physically ready but not "mentally tough enough yet," or another's "smelling" victory, or a team's being "really up for it" abound. Following the recent (1978) Wimbledon semifinals, I counted no fewer than five references to the mental or psychological side of things in the *New York Times* article reporting the event:

"Miss Evert's . . . victory over Billie Jean King was filled with psychological impact. . . . Connors poses a psychological and physical hurdle [to Gerulaitis]. . . . [Mrs. King holds a] mental grip . . . over younger rivals. . . . 'It's very psychological when we play each other,' [Miss Evert] said. . . . 'Psychologically, I'm not as match-tough as I was last year,' [Miss Evert] said." [1]

Amidst all this "psychology" permeating the stadiums, one might well ask whether there are any psychologists in the house, and whether they have anything to contribute beyond the recognition that more seems to pass between players on opposite ends of the court than three tennis balls.

SPORTS PSYCHOLOGY

Some are beginning to appear. So much so that this new field is almost ready to start applying for membership in the indexes of college textbooks, and perhaps as the 39th Division of the American Psychological Association. But the emphasis, it seems to me, is so far misplaced. Coaches are interviewed in an effort to determine what makes them successful, and diet, drug, and recreation habits of players are monitored with extreme care. Things have not yet reached the point of analyzing Billy Martin-Reggie Jackson disputes by reference to the psychological conflicts of Martin's Oedipal stage, but that's coming, I'm sure.[2]

To understand the potential of a psychological inquiry into sports, and why answers are not likely to come from the rather narrow perspective so far taken, it's worthwhile considering for a moment the vastness of the field of psy-

[1] *The New York Times,* July 5, 1978, D11, D14.

[2] And not too slowly. Since writing this, I've discovered a series of letters to *The New York Times* (July 16, 1978, V2) on the Martin affair, some of which suggest that the "real tragedy . . . is the absence of competent psychiatric help for all concerned" and that there is obviously something wrong with our society when a "maladjusted . . . misfit [full of] self-pity" can have so much appeal to "people . . . otherwise warm and social."

chology. While its topology can be variously surveyed, it contains nothing if not extremes. Its methods range from scrupulous, scientific experimentation to personal, therapeutic judgment. While the experimentalist performs surgery on the subcortex of the prepubescent male albino rat to test a hypothesis about sexual arousal, the therapist listens to free associations on the couch about one's mother. Its subject matter ranges from the ancient to the contemporary. Interpretations of the role of Jehovah in Genesis are reported at the same meetings as investigations of the motives behind LSD consumption (some listeners may still be working on the connection). And in its application, psychology ranges from establishing principles of "normalcy" to explaining the behavior of the aberrant. One psychologist in the courtroom testifies to the defendant's mental incapacity while another advises the prosecution on selecting a jury of his peers.

Sports psychology is therefore not quite as new a field as some of its recent attention would suggest. Had we taken notice, we would have found it already spread over the psychological map. Sports are experimental enough to require constant formulation and revision of hypotheses on the playing field, yet clinical enough to encourage traveling counselors for some of the teams; they're contemporary enough to generate front-page headlines, yet have so much of a history that shattering records constitutes part of their drama; and while they're "normal" enough to encourage participation and audiences of hundreds of millions, they're aberrant enough to have produced a legion of superhuman super-heroes. Were sports psychology to become a separate division of the APA, its interests would overlap constantly with those of all other divisions.

Throughout this book, I have made an effort not to restrict myself to a single psychological perspective or methodology, or to consider subject matter that fits only a proscribed area of psychological concern. The resultant chapters bear on issues that can be found in experimental, clinical, social, cognitive, motivational, and personality psychology.

The general purposes are to increase appreciation of the game of tennis and to improve the reader's game, if improvement is sought. I have argued against a number of shibboleths about strategy (e.g., thinking ruins one's game), provided support, when warranted, for commonly heard suggestions (e.g., change your game when losing), elaborated beliefs that have only occasionally been hinted at (e.g., it's difficult to win after a tight battle that you've lost), and proposed helpful rules (e.g., alternate your risk-taking approach to the game often).

And while it all may sound a bit too elaborate for something as simple as tennis, I think sports, and tennis in particular, justify the attention. True, tennis is only a game. But we're only trying to play it.

ALL SPORTS ARE PSYCHOLOGICAL, BUT SOME ARE MORE PSYCHOLOGICAL THAN OTHERS

And tennis is the most. As sports are a unique occasion for play between consenting adults, so tennis is unique among sports. I refer not to such characteristics as the participants' maniacally banging around a ball all morning, or the implications of its historical, aristocratic ancestry (if you think "*lawn* tennis" connotes something fairly well-manicured, you'll be happy to hear the game was first known as "royal tennis"), but rather to its structure and its rules, especially when played at modest levels of proficiency (where one acts as his own referee, for example). Since these characteristics uniquely or strongly apply to tennis, even in relation to other sports, it follows that tennis and psychology are natural playmates.

Tennis is different from other sports in the following ways:

1. Its scoring system is unique. For one thing, it is complicated, existing on three different levels (point, game, set) simultaneously. For a second, it permits a player to lose the majority of points in a match and still win, in much the same manner that a presidential candidate can lose the election even with a majority of the popular vote, if they're not concentrated in the right places. For a third, leads are never as insurmountable as they are in sports where time runs out (football, basketball) or where there is no upper limit to the potential margin of victory (baseball). For a fourth thing, points *count double*. A point lost by one player is a point scored by the other. This is rarely true in other sports. If you fail to convert the field goal, the other team does not get three points, but if you fail to get your serve over the net, your opponent scores. And finally, as a result of these characteristics, the tempo can shift dramatically as a result of minor changes in the score.

2. Offense and defense are closely integrated. It's not as if one team is "up" or has the ball, while the other team is on the field or defending. It may be your turn to hit the ball, but you may be in an extremely defensive position. No one need be overtly on the offensive or defensive as ground strokes get traded. It is not an exception, such as an intercepted pass, that converts a defensive position into an offensive one. When you do "have the ball," you don't have it for very long. A subsidiary, but important, consequence of this lack of critical distinction between offense and defense is that practice periods, not involving one player's hitting while the other fields, are often more fun than playing games. And another is that your equipment must serve both offensive and defensive needs. Your racquet must be both bat and glove.

3. The referee plays a more central role than in most

other sports (with the possible exception of boxing). In tennis, he must decide who gets the point, and a relatively large number of shots are hit close to one of five boundary lines on each side of the court. A basketball referee never has to decide whether the ball actually went in or not (goaltending is about as close as he'll come to that), and even when he's deciding something like whether a player or the ball hit the end line, it's relatively infrequent and doesn't immediately affect the scoring. Similarly, a baseball or football umpire will only very rarely have to decide whether the ball was on the fair or foul side of a foul pole or inside or outside the goal post. Balls and strikes and penalties do get constant attention, and are clearly subject to the errors of judgment and perception that we might expect, but they too are not as directly influential on the score. Perhaps, most importantly, as mentioned above, one acts as his own referee, except at the uppermost levels of play. While schoolyard basketball and football players do too, the absence of any question on most scoring plays suggests that the fact of refereeing is less consequential than in tennis.

4. You're all alone (except in doubles, when you and your partner are all alone). The error is yours alone. There is no team to camouflage or confuse the issue, no receiver or pass-blocker upon whom to deflect responsibility for the interception. While some other sports are "individual" as well, they tend to be mixed with other characteristics not present in tennis. In golf, there is no direct head-to-head competition where your error may be produced by the other's proficiency. And in boxing, you're returning, after each round, to the advice of the manager and of the handler. Occasionally, one finds tennis "coaches," but generally they serve a minor function. In team tennis, they seem mainly to be part of the rooting section and to handle the line-up card. And Ian Tiriac sending cryptic hand signals to Guillermo Vilas between points hardly diminishes

Vilas' solitude on the court. In addition, except at the highest levels, you're playing your lonely game surrounded by others playing theirs. It's like being an only child in a family of ten children.

5. There are many decisions to make and there is not enough time to make them. With only the slightest of alterations in strategy, each point provides you the opportunity to be risky or conservative. Should I try a passing shot or a lob? Should I go for the ace or just get it in? Being "smart" continually looms as an option, hinging often on what the opponent is or is not expecting. While there are unexpected, or smart, or "safe" plays in other sports as well, the options aren't continually flowing as in tennis, with instant change in strategy dictated. Teams can huddle or call time out. The golfer can address and readdress his ball, and continually attempt to assess the wind velocity and direction.

6. Choice of opponents is more open. People of differing abilities can play without the better necessarily feeling compromised. When teams are mismatched in other sports, the game is often no fun at all. Furthermore, the selection of opponents is a natural and constant part of the tennis ritual. Golf may again be similar in that you round up your own party, but since one is largely competing against himself and the scorecard, the others' abilities do not have as direct an effect.

7. It looks easy. The face of the racquet is big and the court is big. In basketball and golf, the goal isn't much bigger than the ball and in baseball the diameter of the bat isn't much different from that of the ball. Judging from those who play the game of tennis, you don't need special genetic endowments or a physical fitness program instituted at age three to do quite well.

8. The game is broken down into many even divisions. You switch serves each game, switch sides every two games, switch direction of serve each point, and get two serves

each time. This produces sixteen different sub-games, each subject to different influences. There are numerous other "even" divisions, such as forehand and backhand, forecourt and backcourt, cross-court and "down the line" shots. "Changing one's game" may sometimes be useful advice, but which game and with what change may not be readily apparent.

9. Tennis is a quiet game. Except for the recently arrived and very different World Team Tennis, and the occasional provocateur in the crowd, there aren't rooting sections and cheerleaders. Much of the play seems to depend on the sound of the racquet meeting the ball, as well as the sight of the ball. And "concentration" seems invariably inter-twined with either silence, or a constant, muted sound pattern. Golf seems the only sport that is similar—one doesn't shout as the player's about to putt—but the absence of directly competing opponents makes the interruption less of an issue than when the opponent in tennis breaks the silence.

Many of these characteristics form the basis for detailed observations throughout the chapters, but it is worthwhile affirming at this point that their existence grants psychology the opportunity to operate with even more room than it does in other sports. Your opponent's inability to amass an insurmountable lead affords some personality types—those who do better in later stages—a chance they otherwise would not have for a comeback (see Chapter 7). Since when you win points is more critical than how many you win, there may be ways of improving your opportunities at critical times through knowledge of the psychological effects of the previous point (Chapter 11). Since rallying is often more fun than playing games, you can indefinitely avoid getting properly prepared (Chapter 6). Being the one to call your opponent's shot "Out!" gives you the chance to feel guilty and her the chance to feel angry (Chapter 4). Since you're all alone out there and very visible to spectators, you may abandon caution prematurely (Chapter 9). Although you're all alone at one side of the court, players on the adjacent ten courts may have a decided effect on your game (Chapter 8). Since there are unexpected dividends to making a "smart" play, learning how biased is that judgment may be helpful (Chapter 10). The opportunity to play with partners of different abilities allows many the option of never getting better (Chapter 5). Since the game looks easy, the importance of missing a shot may be exaggerated (Chapter 2). Since there are so many sub-games, resulting from the necessity to "even" things out, distinguishing the characteristics of what you're doing well in is important (Chapter 6). And since tennis is primarily a quiet game, talking can be very manipulative (Chapter 3).

THE MYSTIQUE OF NATURALISM

Some people may be "natural" athletes, but I've yet to find them. While it's obvious that some body types are more adaptable to some sports than others, it should also be apparent that nobody springs full bloom into the center court of Wimbledon. Even the great "natural" athlete, Evonne Goolagong, discovered in the natural surroundings of the Australian backcountry, had a decade of tutelage by a tennis-school proprietor before her meteoric rise to the top as a teenager.

A recent work on tennis,[3] by emphasizing the distinction between the "inner" and "outer" games, returns us to this misguided domain of naturalism and deserves some attention. The author can be congratulated for having officially

[3] W. T. Gallwey. *The Inner Game of Tennis.* (New York: Random House, 1974.)

opened to examination the "mental" side of tennis, and some players may have profited by redirecting their improvement efforts. The danger, however, in this emphasis on the "inner" prescription is sharing the conclusion that if the source of the difficulties is not the knees or the feet, it must be the head. We are thus advised, in effect, to "get out of" our heads, to let our natural, rhythmic selves gain expression, to stop thinking and simply "be."

Such belief in the grand, instinctual reservoir of human potential, polluted by careful, methodical instruction, can be traced historically, and systematized politically, philosophically, and poetically. I won't do all that, but will quickly mention some contemporary representatives of this theme because they do have widespread appeal. To gestalt therapists, "The intellect is the whore of intelligence";[4] to Rudolph Steiner-ites, a child, approaching elementary education, should be prevented from reading before six or seven, even if he or she expresses an interest or capability, because it would interfere with his or her natural powers of wonder or something; to the wide receiver on the San Francisco 49ers, press inquiries like how did you get so cleanly away from the cornerback on the deciding touchdown pass deserve the response, "I dunno, I just catches 'em, I let somebody else figure out how"; to a growing, militant band of college professors, all instruction referring to something happening before 1968 is an elitist demonstration of irrelevance; and to some confused tennis commentators on television, since if you're playing well, you don't want to think, "The top players will tell you that when they begin to think, they begin to lose."

Rather than being representative of what psychology's all about, this naturalistic "mindlessness" is simply silly. Surely

[4] F. Perls. *Gestalt Therapy Verbatim* (Toronto, New York, and London: Bantam, 1971), p. 24.

the intellect can get in the way;[5] when the fingers are danc-
ing on the keyboard, who wants to think which one is doing
what? In the process of trying to recall something, we might
not properly attend to what is present, or in thinking about
what went wrong, we might become too self-conscious and
not conscious of what's around us. But to conclude from
these possibilities that the trouble is mainly in the head
is to take a relatively minor portion of human activity—
that which, in fact, is probably so well learned that it can
be performed smoothly, without thought, like the centipede's walking—and elevate it to universal stature. Not all
driving is cruising along an empty highway at an even
speed. Much of it has to do with hustling around for a parking place while not shooting a red light, while not knocking
anybody over, while switching back and forth a few times
between lanes, while seeing out of the back window who
just left the curb. And while such attention can certainly
impede the effortless, flowing character of your cruising,
not being attentive to all these conditions may leave you
circling the block endlessly. The "inner" prescription may
have some uses, but only if you never play a game and if all
you want to do is to escape complexity.

In tennis your opponent is a problem, and it may be to
your advantage to notice what he's up to. Certain changes
in strategy are indicated at certain points, and to recognize
those points takes an awareness of something other than the
clouds, the patterns of light and dark, or the rhythmic,
natural cadence of the ball bouncing on the cement. A re-
peated failure to do something, like make game point,
might be the result of some characteristic that displays it-

---

[5] The centipede was happy, quite,/Until a toad in fun/Said 'Pray,
which leg goes after which?'/This worked his mind to such a pitch,/He
lay distracted in a ditch,/Considering how to run." (A. Watts. *The Way
of Zen* [New York: Pantheon, 1957], p. 27.)

self in that pattern, but you have little chance of altering it if even the pattern goes unrecognized. In fact, not only does thinking not ruin one's game, not only does it afford the opportunity of vastly improving one's game, it is implicitly recognized as offering that potential even by those who advocate quite the opposite.

What else can be taken to be the meaning behind the well-known strategy of changing your game when losing? The same commentator who announces the business about thinking getting in the way will also pronounce this one, with predictable regularity. And the implications—this myth happens generally to be true—are that you must recognize what you're doing and do something different. This double task can hardly occur if you are just "being," or doing what comes naturally. Connors would not have been serving his second ball from the deuce court to Laver's forehand if he hadn't suddenly realized that Laver's propensity is to rush the net on second serve—but only off his backhand. Just because you may not want to think when you're playing well does not imply that if you start to think, you will begin to lose. Indeed, thinking is just what Connors began doing, to his advantage, in order not to lose.

The tendency to opt for the "mindless" strategy is quite strong, and certainly psychologically understandable. Using one's head means attention, memory, and work. Not everyone is willing to give that much. Not everyone has a warm relationship with his or her thinking processes. (Leave me alone—I just want to have fun!) And certainly everyone, at one time or another, has enough to think about without looking for trouble on the tennis court, too. Yet, recognizing the appeal of the pundits of "mindlessness" also gives you the chance to ask yourself just what are the characteristics of your own thinking process? Do you really hate it that much? Is it really no fun to think about things, and then perhaps find, from the manifold possibilities opened up, that it is intrinsically enjoyable to solve a problem that you have thought about? Is there no thrill in doing the unexpected, and seeing it work to your advantage? When taking a smart shot on the tennis court, are you really depleted by all the energy that went into figuring it out, or are you not; in fact, further energized by it?

Finally, if understanding why the "natural" crowd has appeal (thinking sounds hard compared to "being") is not sufficient to raise all eyebrows over the worth of its advice, then the recognition that its message is intrinsically contradictory ought to end all doubts. If thought is the enemy of performance, how is it that we can profit from hearing this? Aren't we thinking about the intrusion of thought? Heeding prescriptions about the inner self is like reading a book that expounds the thesis that we can't learn anything from books. In short, the teachers of "naturalism" imply by their works that being natural ain't all that natural, and being taught ain't all that corrupting.

As I will argue throughout this book, success on the next tennis point is determined not by emptying your mind, but rather by whether you're planning to be risky or conservative, what you think about your chances, whether you're afraid of losing your friends, the smile on your opponent's face, how guilty you feel about your last line call, who won the last point, how he or she won it, what the score is, what the score was one and two points ago, which of the sixteen possible games is about to be played, what your opponent is chattering about, what you think about his or her chatter, who's watching, whether you're an introvert or an extrovert, whether you can tolerate your own mistakes, how assertive you've been, what the players on the next court are up to, and, once in a while, who has the stronger forehand. No wonder the proponents of "naturalism" have a certain appeal.

I will make one concession to them. We all do have

enough to think about. I am the last person, even were I sure of the absolute truth of all I say here, to put each conclusion into constant practice (a fact which may explain something about my failure to reach Wimbledon again this year and, I dare say, next year as well). Select. Try out some observations and ideas. As being blissfully ignorant is an escape that doesn't work to our own best advantage, so is being overeducated. "Wait a minute," he says in bed, quickly riffling through the pages of his sex manual to find the appropriate spot. At least leave your notes in the locker room when you go out on the court, or you may find that while you're looking up that part about when to come to the net, you're getting passed.

CHAPTER 2

Rational Therapy: It's a Mistake to Be Perfect

Slowly, painstakingly, Daniel starts making the loop, comes back roughly to where he started, begins a relatively straight, vertical line that extends about two thirds of the way toward the next line, and moves back to examine his "p." Content, he continues with similar concentration on his "q," "r," and "s." Suddenly, realizing his "s" is facing the wrong direction, he throws the pencil down, crumples up his sheet of paper, and dashes off to tell his mommy he messed up.

Slowly, methodically, Daniel's father bends his knees, keeps his eye on the ball, brings his racquet back, shifts his weight from his back to his forward foot, swings, and sends the ball into the net. With an impassioned cry, he flings the racquet after the ball and dashes off the court to get a drink.

How far can the tree grow from the apple? Since Daniel's only six, he will probably not bear so many scars from that immediate experience the next time he sits down to write. But when the situation again arises for his father, he may be sure to "choke" or get "tentative," since he knows too well that the knee-bending and weight-shifting attention are secondary to his recollection of what happened.

A basic precept of Rational Psychotherapy (sometimes referred to as Rational-Emotive Therapy, or RET) is that underlying most behavioral and emotional distress is the belief, "I must be perfect." From that irrational thought follows a closely aligned one: "It would be terrible if I made a mistake." Behind all emotional problems there must be some irrational belief, and those head the list.

On the tennis court, critical points are often missed. The circumstance is one of the most familiar to players or spectators. Biggest point of the match. Set point against you on your own serve. And for the first time in the match you double-fault. The one occasion on which you least want to do it, the one occasion on which you are so conscious of not trying to do anything special with the serve lest you give it away too readily, and the one occasion on which you make the error.

A case of nerves? Too much tension? Sure, but that requires further analysis if one is going to get anywhere with it. "I better not make the mistake" is the implicit belief of one who makes the mistake. Critical points are missed because they're treated as overwhelmingly important. There is probably no greater way to produce an error than to think, "It would be terrible if I made an error here."

Ironically, such a belief is held most of all by those who are losing. The leader can say more easily, "I make errors." His stature is evident to his opponent, the spectators, and himself. When one is losing, he fears his power may be not at all evident. To accept his errors, then, may be an admission that he's not really so good. The winner doesn't have that fear, because the proof that he is good is there—he is winning. The loser must therefore proclaim his surprise at his error, with as many histrionics as the audience will bear. "I just don't believe it. Did you see that shot I just missed? Why, my grandmother could have made it blindfolded." It's not the winner who throws the racquet upon making an error. And, not fearing that his imperfections signify that he's no good at all, the favorite doesn't double-fault at critical times.

Is the irrational belief in perfection, which can be responsible for "choking," unique to tennis? Not at all, for certainly one hears about blowing the golden opportunity in other sports as well. Two foul shots missed in the final seconds. The three-foot putt blown on the final green. The winning touchdown pass dropped in the end zone at the buzzer. But notice that each of these examples, even in the team sports, illustrates what is always true in tennis—that you're all alone. The error is more likely to be made when you alone are responsible for it, since there is no way to diffuse blame. It is less likely to be made in a team sport, where, if it is made, it is not as easy to see who made it. The irrational belief, therefore, that it would be terrible if I missed these foul shots or this putt or this overhead is responsible in those instances for just what is feared.

A second reason for the greater applicability of the problems of perfectionism in tennis is that the sport looks easy. Your grandmother might very well have made the easy approach shot you overhit by twelve feet, even if she never sunk a basket or a putt in her life. Certainly, the sport would have proven much less popular had people who started to play really known how hard it was to be good at it. But everyone thinks he can do it. A big racquet and a big court. And even though the stars look pretty trim and fit, in more earthly surroundings it is clear that not all players have given up sybaritic pleasures for the season. To miss an ordinary, forehand ground stroke, therefore, is to miss something that you know someone else can hit over the net fifty times in a row during his drill sessions. Even at stratospheric levels of accomplishment, nobody expects you to make fifty foul shots in a row.

On each point of a match, there is a winner and a loser. Yet, if you watch the match closely, there is practically always a time after which the eventual loser becomes dismayed, is evidently disgusted with himself, looks pained, shakes his head, stares at the ground, and sometimes wears a mocking smile which suggests that no one has ever played so badly. Or he displays a certain bravado which sends him suddenly back to the baseline with an air of lightness, and a let's-get-this-farce-over-with movement. We have all seen it or exhibited it. And if the opponent is not so lucky, he's ducking the balls that are being knocked all over the place—or, with the more dramatic losers, the racquet itself.

Some illustrations will support the observation that the irrational belief in the necessity for perfection is most applicable to the game of tennis. Although double-faults at critical moments of professional matches are well known, further examples of "the pressure getting to him" keep occurring. But the pressure, such as it is, only gets to the underdog; the winner, not having to treat his errors so critically, makes less of them.

Tanner against Connors in a WCT event of 1978: a match in which the "new" Tanner is being displayed. He's been developing a top-spin ground stroke, and is being coached by Dennis Ralston, former Davis Cup captain. Connors is the big favorite, but Tanner is holding his own at 4–4. Suddenly, for the first time in the match, he falls behind, 15–30. The next point he double-faults. Not match point, not even game point, but the first point against a favored opponent that you feel you must win. Connors won the game and the set, after that 40–15 advantage— just what Tanner was probably thinking would happen if he lost that point, just what made him lose the point.

Gerulaitis-Laver in the round robin, 1978 WCTs, a $320,000 tournament. Gerulaitis needed only to beat Laver to enter the semifinals. But while Gerulaitis was favored (this was thirty-eight-year-old, not vintage, Laver), the match was very close. The deciding third set went to a tie-breaker, and Gerulaitis double-faulted on his last two serves, the final one at 5–6, to lose the match. (His previous serve was at 5–3 and if won would have given him three match points.) Does this seem contrary to what was said about the double-fault affecting the underdog? The point at which the favored player is no longer the favorite is the point at which he feels he cannot afford to lose that point or his reign is over. For winners can always afford to lose. When Gerulaitis had been unable to prove himself superior, to such an extent that he realized he could lose the match, Laver became the favored player. And so Gerulaitis "choked" when he started believing it would be terrible if he lost.

In the U.S. Open of 1975, during the early rounds of the Connors-Borg rivalry, Borg lost by the interesting score of 7–5, 7–5, 7–5. There is only one way for a 7–5 score to result. There must be a tie at 5-all, and then a break in serve in the 11th or 12th game. Since Connors had served first, that means that *in each set*, Borg was broken in the last game, with the score 5–6. Borg lost the game which, if won, would bring them both to a tie-breaker. Borg lost the game he could least afford to, the one which, if lost, would cost him the set immediately. Borg lost the set on his own serve, although he had been even on serve with Connors up to that point. And he did it three consecutive times. Borg, by the way, was the underdog, it being a couple of years before he really came into his own. But, as the score suggests, the decisive factor in the match was not ability, but Borg's believing that he better not lose that game and in each case then doing it.

The fundamental characteristic of most irrational beliefs is their exaggeration. There is nothing irrational in being disappointed if things don't work out the way you would have liked, but there is a lot irrational in being devastated. The severity of the disappointment comes from the belief that things must work out the way you planned. Were there no imperative, were it viewed as simply desirable for things to work out your way, there would be no devastation. Basic to rational psychotherapy is the attempt to replace the irrational belief—"Things must go the way I want"—with the rational one that it would be nice if they did.

Double-faults occur because of the exaggerated belief, "I must do it this time or I won't get another chance." That is the root of the pressure that so often results in great stress and poor performance. Cure the tendency to exaggerate and you'll cure the "choking." A beginning is to ask yourself how it is you seem to "choke" so often, if you "must do it" each particular time. There are a lot of "last chances" that seem to come up.

The Last Chance syndrome is responsible for diminishing one's effectiveness in a number of areas. Not being desperate or nervous enough to think that this is the last job for which you'll have a decent chance, or that this is the last person who will ever consider you worthwhile enough to treat seriously, will increase your chances of success. Therapy consists of substituting the rational belief, "It would be nice to get it, but there will be other occasions." Otherwise, the cycle cannot be broken. Because you've lost job opportunities (each of which you regarded as your Last Chance), you become intolerant of your mistakes, extremely nervous at the next interview, and likely to interpret practically anything as a sign of imperfection. This reduces further your chances of success.

Perfectionism is debilitating in a number of other ways. It increases the tendency to procrastinate. Not wanting to go beyond the last opportunity, you delay the critical moment sufficiently to minimize chances of success. If this is really your last chance to get a grade of "A," if your failure in this course would really be so terrible since you'll never be that close to your goal again, then it's understandable why you never sit down to write the paper until it's too late to get the "A." Having then to do your work so hurriedly, you have excused the failure to meet expectations.

A second effect is to make you excessively cautious about undertaking some activity. If you'll never meet anyone as nice or attractive, if he or she is the last opportunity you'll have, if it would be terrible if he or she didn't respond to your overture, then you will be understandably timid about extending an invitation. And, equally probably, Last Chance perfectionism may lead you to take excessive risks. A sure sign that things are too important is demonstrably dismissing their importance. The one who values his life so highly that he doesn't know which way to turn is the one determined to take it into his own hands as he recklessly seemingly seeks to end it. Throwing yourself at the potential companion, prematurely and inappropriately, is probably not only doomed to fail but an unmistakable sign that failure has become too important.

Exaggerated delay, in relation to tennis, is often exhibited in those who never seem to find the time to learn or to improve their game. (Some related, irrational exaggerations will be discussed in the next paragraph.) Exaggerated risk and caution are present continually in matches, and will be discussed in detail in Chapter 9.

IRRATIONAL BELIEFS COMMON TO TENNIS PLAYERS

Anyone intent on discovering the irrationality of his belief system on the tennis court would have no trouble coming up with an extensive list of his or her own favorites. Here are some common ones:

1. *I must catch on quickly.*

Apparent reasons for not playing the game at all or for not taking it seriously oftentimes mask this one. It's a simple enough game, or so it appears. What is there to it except hitting a ball onto a big playing area? Therefore, the frustration evident in those who fail to pick it up quickly (especially big, bruising men who normally pride themselves on being athletic, or slight women who think they could never do anything athletic) makes them give it up entirely. It then gets referred to as a silly pastime or another indication of the overemphasis in our society on competitiveness. People who delay starting or improving their game may have gotten the hint that they won't become No. 1 at Forest Hills so quickly, and may feel that that would be terrible. Perhaps the people I refer to in the Preface who refuse to get out there with any competitive interest expected to be better more quickly. That may be partly because they had great expectations about themselves, and partly because they underestimated the difficulty of the game.

2. *I shouldn't miss an easy shot.*

We all know it's bound to happen, except when it happens to us. How often have you seen someone miss an overhead, especially a short one, or a volley when the court was wide open, or a serve that is not to one side or the other, and then walk back to the baseline for the next point without some dramatic exhibition? And if you're thinking of someone who can do that, you're probably thinking of either someone who can't distinguish easy from hard or someone who does quite well for herself, since she isn't handicapped by irrational thinking. Indeed, so rare is this quality of calmness after these shots are missed, that in imagining it, you might become aware of how powerful an effect it would have on you, the opponent. You don't know what she's thinking! She hasn't displayed the histrionics, the belief in her perfection. She thus hasn't enabled you to dismiss her act. She remains a mystery.

3. *I must take advantage of every opportunity.*

Although it is similar to the first irrational belief above, this one is more general. There are many opportunities that offer advantages in the course of a match or a point. Not only easy shots, but shots worked up to, shots to work on (like an approach shot), easy opponents, big leads— each affords you the chance to win, and the chance to feel terrible if you miss out. If the opportunity for a winning game is lost, the effects are severe, because of the irrational belief that you must take advantage when you can. For this reason, the loss of a 40–0 lead is critical. Similarly, a reason why a long point that is eventually lost is significant is that at some time during the point, you probably had the chance to win it. And if you're in danger of losing to someone you should beat, you often do as soon as you realize it.

4. *I should never look outplayed.*

If you're driven off the court, it must be that your opponent is lucky or you're really having an "off day," or that something with the equipment is weird. Rationalizations for a lost point or game or match come complete with gestures, the picture conveying anything but that you can lose honestly with your best effort. To see this belief as a derivative of perfectionism, one need only reflect on what occurs when the rationalizations are impossible, when one has unmistakably been outplayed. Then one is likely to conclude that he must be no good at all.

One of the advantages I have always had as a tennis player is my defensive style. People notice the outright winner, but not as readily the consistent retrieving, so that the defensive player has the advantage of never quite looking as good as he is. Those who would lose to me would often tell themselves they must have been no good at all. Such opponents would feel much better on seeing me beat somebody else I wasn't supposed to, since that partially dispelled the belief that they were so terrible. Furthermore, such witnessing of a match I would have with another often marked the point at which the original, defeated opponent would be able to come back and beat me, his enlarged perspective on my disguised capability serving to make him less hard on himself.

5. *There's always one right shot to hit.*

This is a derivative of the general, irrational belief that there's always one right answer to a problem. It has two devastating consequences. One is to persist too long with something that succeeds. The other is to give up too early something that fails. Hitting my first serve to my opponent's backhand in the ad court, and winning with it the first two times, I was almost finished with the match before I realized I had been losing all my subsequent points on that side. He had adjusted, as well he should, by moving a step to his left, and I had continued to serve wide. Not only is there more than one right answer at a time, but in situations where the other is in constant opposition to you, what is right is guaranteed not to be right forever. Or wrong. If the receiver returns a serve to his forehand well, the server often decides too quickly not to go there anymore. Maybe he normally swings too early and guessed wrong this time, delaying him just enough to be timely. In fact, a good return off forehand and backhand is often all one needs to begin moving toward victory, since the opponent is likely to conclude there's nowhere else to go.

The belief is still irrational, even in cases where there's a definite weakness or strength of the opponent. If it's right to play to it, it won't be right forever, and the same holds for avoiding it. A weak backhand should be run around sometimes; this can be done more successfully if you anticipate the direction of the opponent's shot. Even when something works, you need to change it. The bluff in poker keeps the other fellow "honest." Otherwise, your expected move reaps no reward, since all respond to it by folding their cards. And eventually, as Connors used to remark about everyone keeping the ball to his forehand to avoid his powerful backhand, you succeed in strengthening the opponent's weakness by continuing to try to use it to your advantage.

6. *Anything that goes wrong is my fault.*

The extreme form of this belief, sometimes referred to as "personalization," is thinking yourself responsible for the flu epidemic, since you were the first to have symptoms. You dash across neighboring courts to retrieve the ball your opponent has mishit, knowing that he saved it from clearing the fence on his side, since your shot was too deep. You say "sorry" if your volleys, in rallying, are too well-angled, even though you've saved your opponent's overhit passing shot. You apologize for not giving your opponent more of a game, when you lose, knowing that he's been bored, however close the score. You apologize for your double-faults. You apologize for your lucky shots, when you win, assuring your opponent that talent will surely reveal itself next time. As the discussion of etiquette, assertion, and nonassertion in Chapter 8 emphasizes, there is plenty of opportunity on the court to do the right thing and an infinite number of ways to do something wrong. But there are also plenty of occasions on which your opponent's mistakes or the world's vicissitudes are simply not your own personal responsibility. It's not your fault, if you overslept, should you get injured by a helicopter crashing through your bedroom ceiling.

7. *I can only do what I feel like doing.*

On the one hand, this is a residue of early childhood (but I don't *feel* like it, Mommy); on the other, it's typically found in hypochondriacs who, by managing to notice their real or imagined symptoms, find ways of opting out of activities because of their feelings; on the third hand, it's an unfortunate result of recent tendencies to get in closer touch with one's feelings, so that people who've acquired some insightful knowledge of themselves irrationally conclude that if you do it when you don't feel like it you're out of touch; and on the fourth hand, it's relatively subtle and often escapes notice as a widespread irrational belief. Self-expression and look-out-for-number-one boys to the contrary, our feelings range in intensity. To insist on really feeling like doing whatever you're doing is to present an unrealistic, perfectionist standard. Once on the tennis court, very few people look like they're suffering, even those who didn't really feel like playing or didn't feel like playing with these opponents. Waiting until you're really "up" for it usually masks the reluctance you have to get better, to work hard, to face embarrassment, or to give up other pursuits. Many a writer—and writers are notorious for never wanting to sit down and write—is well advised just to go over there and do a little, even if he doesn't feel like it. Hit a few keys, don't make it your best day. And voila! The feeling dissipates, and one carries on in much the same manner as if he "really felt like it." I'm not advocating going out and playing when your blisters and knees and elbows are screaming "No!" but if you've started regular tennis and then stopped, not "feeling like it," or if you have no discernible physical ailments but just have funny feelings acting up, or if your opportunities for getting better are often pushed to the background by other activities, you might ask yourself why your interest is still there. The continual battle implies that something is strong enough not to be so easily avoided.

8. *I could be really good if I tried.*

Maybe you could, maybe you couldn't, but all that this particular belief contributes is to justify not trying, not practicing, not taking your endeavors seriously. While I believe there's quite a bit to learn about in this game, some of which might even be found in these pages, I am not so perfectionist to believe that everyone could profit, if they only wanted to. Not enough is known about behavior for anyone to be quite that glib, and sometimes activities are too complex or difficult to warrant further attention. If we find ourselves continually upset at our lack of progress or enjoyment, despite everyone's advice, we might do well to leave it. Work on yourself, but don't use this sensible advice as a way of ignoring what goes on in the world. I'm not sure how to distinguish the extreme form of tennis-avoidance, but if you really never could stand sports, and now steadfastly refuse to change, if you're really forcing yourself to continue reading because you know you should really find out why you hate the game, then maybe you have enough clues indicating that you should give it up. It may often be possible to change by changing your cognitions, but it's often easier to change your world. It's something that not all psychologists will remind you of, since then it might turn out that you don't need them around so much.

In fact, this really-good-if-I-tried irrationality underlies a great deal of rationalizing in any profession. It's a common irrational belief of psychologists that they understand anything anyone does. (Can you picture a psychologist being surprised rather than smugly nodding? Or saying, "Really! You didn't!"?) And it's a common irrational belief of writers that they can so illuminate their subject matter that everyone would be able to see the light, if only everybody were willing to be so illuminated. (Can you picture a writer saying, "I don't know; I just can't explain it"?) The rationalization may be what keeps a lot of us going, but it also may be what stops a good many of us from humbly appreciating the limits of our expertise and craft.

9. *I'm no good at all.*

Intrinsic to the variety of irrational beliefs so far presented is what RET practitioners sometimes refer to as "awfulizing." Applied to oneself, the derivative irrational belief is, "I'm just no good." I wanted to win, I didn't get what I wanted, so I'm no good at all. Disputing this irrational belief can serve as a model for trying to dispense with the others—which are all intimately connected—and can introduce the kind of cognitive therapy, therapy based on thinking, that often results from the analysis.

As mentioned earlier, therapy largely consists of disputing the irrational belief and trying to replace it with a more rational one. (It would not be terrible if you didn't get the job, it would just be unfortunate.) Disputing the generalized belief that "I'm just no good" consists of trying to offer examples that dispute it and having the client generate his own. An example from my own tennis experience could serve to illustrate how this can come about naturally.

The first time I played on a "tennis ladder" in my local public courts, I went through a period of losing some nine matches in a row. This is the kind of event that can prevent one from ever showing his face at the court again. (Hey, whatever happened to Charlie? We never see him around here anymore. Oh, Charlie, he plays at Central Park now. Yeah, he says the courts are more to his liking.) The reason that the losses didn't affect me adversely, and that I was able to keep playing until I won, was simple. I had won the first two matches I had played. As a relatively unknown player on these courts, especially against two flashier, high-ranked opponents, the early victories provided me the opportunity to withstand the future losses. I was, in effect, prevented from believing "I'm no good at all" by the earlier victories. Otherwise, I'm fairly sure, I would have been strongly tempted to flee to the countryside for relative anonymity, or at least to continue in my previous ways of only rallying and not playing sets, since it would have been evident that "Something happens to me when I play games."

The experience of success provided me the means to avoid exaggerating the failure (even though the latter, by a score of 9–2, was more extensive than the former). Those odds, by the way, have significance too. The fact that I lost so many more than I won did not impair my standing, since victories carry me up five rungs and losses only bring me down one. Funny tennis-ladders or not, such odds do reflect the relative effects of success and failure, if you're trying new things. It needn't matter that you've failed at twenty job interviews; all it takes is one success.

Increasing attention to appropriately positive material will work in other, more specific instances as well. To recognize that you missed a shot not because you're so terrible or don't have it today, but because he hit a very good return can be very calming. By discriminating your error from your opponent's winner, you decrease the likelihood of considering everything that doesn't go your way as so awful.

COGNITIVE APPROACHES TO THERAPY

Rational Psychotherapy is a type of cognitive approach to the diagnosis of personality and performance. Like other cognitive theories and methods, it puts a heavy emphasis on thinking, both as the source of the problem and the potential cure. (As distinguished, for example, from psychoanalytic thought, which would consider "personalizing" to be the expression of a repressed wish to have great power or control. Who else but the one ruling the world in fantasy could think his flu so important as to be caught by everyone?) Replace irrational thoughts with rational ones and all things will be rendered unto you. Well, if not all that, at least you won't be so upset much of the time.

There are two other aspects of the cognitive approach that have special relevance to tennis-playing, and I want to touch on them briefly. The first is the proposition that the mere absence of thought, rather than exaggerated or irrational thinking, can reduce one's best effort. Clinicians sometimes report this phenomenon in the case of severe antisocial behavior. Thought often seems to stop with the crime and its potential rewards. The criminal pays no attention to consequences if he is caught.

Not enough thought is given by tennis players to particular patterns of play that have evolved and are likely to evolve in their current play. In fact, it is surprising how few otherwise sophisticated people think ahead on the tennis court. It's as if they are so interested in not making a mistake that they consider it a significant victory merely to get the ball back this time, or else they are so demanding of themselves that they fail to see why every shot will not end the rally for them.

Think a shot ahead. If I return serve to his forehand, where is he likely to put it? And what will I do then? Did the last point that I won off his serve not have a particular pattern worth remembering? If nothing else, thinking ahead prevents errors that often result from indecision, from selecting at the last moment a shot that you were not prepared to take.

There are many opportunities in tennis for being thoughtful. Not quite as many as in chess, perhaps, since you're the only piece you're moving around the board, but enough. (White's cross-court drop-shot refused! A significant opening.) Providing appropriate thoughts in tennis contexts where none were evident is part of this book's purpose.

The final area within the cognitive domain that deserves mention is that of imagery. The assumption behind its use is quite simple. Often the deficiency in performance may be traced to not having an image of being successful. Perhaps the inability to perform delicate brain surgery is not totally explicable by this deficiency in "imaging," but a lot else is. The hesitancy to pursue something one wants, it sometimes turns out, is fostered by having no image of getting what one wants. There are thus two therapeutic possibilities. One is to imagine in as much detail as possible getting what you want; the second is to try to imagine not getting what you want and experiencing an appropriate, unexaggerated feeling along with it.

There is the strong possibility, for example, that some sexual difficulties may be caused by having no image of success. The image itself might be too graphic and frightening, or there might simply be an ignorance of technique. Picturing oneself, therefore, in the act of doing something that one may want to (or that one's partner wants him to), but about which one is somewhat "hung up," may be a first step toward being able to overcome the difficulty.

If one can "image" successfully, but only experiences dread in association with the image, then a second technique is to conceive of the dreaded image, and then imagine a more appropriate affect. To many overeaters, the worst thing they can imagine is abstaining while others about them are indulging their appetites on succulent morsels. By picturing the scene as graphically as they can, and then imagining an experience of slight disappointment rather than of dread, and finally contemplating an experience of enjoyment connected to the picture, they can make progress. This can be encouraged by imagining positive aspects of the scene—the slimmer waistline which others may admire, the social conversation at the gathering. It turns out that the dread of being unable to withstand refraining from eating while others are satisfying their appetites is often at the root of obesity.

I have had this experience on the tennis court: I watched someone with a good serve play a match and discovered that I was serving much better. I did this without being conscious of having recorded something of his form or of having tried to imitate any part of it. I did not know whether I was tossing the ball higher than usual or twisting my torso more. But I did discover that I had been carrying around a mental image of his serve—an image that seemed to appear spontaneously just prior to my own serve. The startling part was that the image was working to my advantage, and on subsequent occasions I could make use of it by calling the image to mind.

It follows from the use of imagery in Cognitive Therapy that the mind can play yet another active role in improving one's tennis game. Especially with the serve, when no other shot must be played before, picture yourself doing it and you'll do it well. Picture the ball falling in where you want it, close to one sideline or the other, and you'll be better able to serve it to either corner. It seems as if the failure to do as well as one might may well correspond to or even be caused by having no image of the goal.

If that technique isn't simple enough, try the alternative technique of picturing what you don't want and changing the feeling that you expect goes along with it. Picture yourself missing the easiest of shots, a short overhead at the net, and then calmly walking back to the baseline. Picture yourself missing the return of serve down the middle and then shrugging it off, rather than throwing the racquet. You may be terrified of such a picture, as if the thought could encourage the reality. And indeed it might. But the chance of making one more error ultimately has less significance than the opportunity of reconstructing one's reactions to them.

CHAPTER 3

"Psyching": The Best Offense Is a Good Defense

Many of us can recall that when Bobby Fischer played Boris Spassky for the World Chess Title in 1972, Fischer kicked up quite a fuss. The lighting was too dim, the board too high, the squares too large. For those of us who might have been inclined to think that chess, of all things, drew its combatants into arenas beyond such mundane concerns, Fischer was quite a shock. The *enfant terrible* of the mental aristocrats, it certainly seemed.

The press and the public even went further, and treated Fischer's constant complaints as an effort to "psych out" the opposition. If psychologists had been consulted on the subject, they would have referred to these antics as a never-outgrown adolescence, a result of the exhibitionist's fixation about calling attention to his own stature or importance. Fischer's behavior obviously illustrated a fundamental defense against one's own feelings of insignificance; the will to power emerges from an image of worthlessness. Even amidst the normally staid chess community, there was overt discomfort at their representative, this hustler polluting the rarefied atmosphere. Such a shame, too, for if he got down to playing, there would really be no one better.

If one looks at the World Title match six years later, one would have to realize that Fischer not only got down to playing that match quite successfully, but that he had quite an impact in gaining consideration of the "minor" playing conditions that he was continually ranting about. It is now a commonplace to hear about such conditions as the height of the chairs and what flavor Anatoly Karpov's yogurt must be. It was even reported that neither Karpov nor Viktor Korchnoi called a day off after the second adjournment of the grueling fifth game because the match had become a "macho" affair in which neither player wished to admit his fatigue by being the one to ask.[1] So much for Queen's Gambit Declined determining the winner!

This shift in chess consciousness illustrates two fundamental and related truths about competition. The first is that there are more transactions between opposing players than those occurring on the playing field and governed by the rules. And the second is that knowledge of these dimensions of interaction does not necessarily give one an unfair advantage, but ignorance of them can certainly put one at a severe disadvantage.

Bobby Fischer's temperamental outbursts may have looked to all the world like an attempt to hustle or intimidate his opponent, but I submit that anyone who would forfeit an entire game, as did Fischer at the beginning of that match, to make a point, must have a considerable point to make. That point often looks like an attempt to intimidate the other. It looks like it because it strategically addresses certain aspects of the game that are also addressed by those who would manipulate. Yet, being alert to the manifold appearances of such manipulations, especially the subtle ways in which those accomplished at it often ply their trade, is sometimes the only way to resist such manipulation. It was not Fischer's country; it was not his chess set. He couldn't even be guaranteed a proper soft drink at his side. When they started constructing special rooms for him

---

[1] *The New York Times*, July 30, 1978, I24.

to play in, it was the least he could do to pay the postage for delivery of his favorite chair from Brooklyn.

Using "psychology" is often seductive, because it conveys the impression of being able to get what you want through the advantage that psychological knowledge may provide. Cultivate a "line" for better results in the art of appealing to members of the opposite sex. Flatter your customers, if you wish them to return. Build in coffee breaks and ping-pong tables, if you want your factory workers to produce more. Perceive other people's needs, attend to them, and you'll get what you want: this advice reflects a popular conception of psychology.

The distinction is of paramount importance. To prevent oneself from being exploited by flatterers, seducers, shoe salesmen, efficiency experts, Russian chessboards, and the opponent across the net is one of psychology's purposes. In frequent reaction to others' efforts to exploit, its aim is to free, not to exploit. It assumes an essentially defensive posture.

Making use of psychology in playing tennis does not mean "socking it to your opponent" by "psyching him out." It does not mean winning, when you're not really better, by "using a little psychology." It does not mean figuring out what others' weaknesses are and then exploiting them to your advantage.

It means offering resistance to being "psyched out"—by your opponent, the conditions of play, or yourself. It means not losing, when you really are better. It means determining what your strengths are and then using them to your advantage.

Failure to appreciate this distinction is why shoe salesmen and efficiency experts give psychology a bad name, and why we often prevent ourselves from greater attainment. We fear identification with the intimidators. Defending ourselves, however, is not equivalent to offending others. It's one thing to kick over your opponent's can of water as you change sides. It's another to bring your own orange juice.

In one of my bigger matches of last year (a decidedly relative term: I was playing for undisputed supremacy of West 103rd Street, between Broadway and Riverside Drive, north side of the block), I clearly remember the turning point. Just after I had hit a strong drive to my opponent's backhand, a ball from another court rolled onto ours, he called time, and we had to do the whole thing over. Up until then, the match had been fairly even. Following that, I lost in straight sets and never posed much of a threat.

Had the situation been clearer, there would have been no problem. Had I just smashed an overhead which he had no chance of returning, other court's ball or no other court's ball, he wouldn't have been able to call time. Had we been exchanging drives from the baseline, with neither player having a discernible advantage, there would similarly have been no problem. We could have either continued or stopped, with no onus attached to the latter. The situation, as it occurred, presented the maximum opportunity for me to be done in, if I both couldn't ignore it and couldn't resolve it. I felt taken advantage of without its being clear that I had been.

I have tried to catalogue, at least in a general way, occurrences of similar types on the court, by which I mean interactions beyond the movement of the chess pieces or the pace and direction of the tennis ball. There are many. Incredibly many. I am no longer surprised when I see a match determined by something of this nature. In fact, I have concluded that *most of them are*, unless players are of totally distinct ability.

While competition in many areas lends itself to this sort

of "outside" influence, tennis is particularly susceptible. There is no umpire to call time because someone has thrown a balloon onto the playing field. There is no team with so clear a possession of the ball that, after an untoward interruption, it could be given it back. The point had to start again; any advantage I had gained by my "offensive" shot could not be claimed.

But why such a "turning point" from such an incident? A clinical psychologist would reason that the internalized anger resulting from an unexpressed feeling of being exploited begins to burn you up. As a result of that anger, some of your cognitions—memory, thinking, perception—are affected for the worse. Some form of arousal can facilitate performance (as will be discussed in the next chapter), but not in the extreme and not while it is being unacknowledged. If you're seeing red, you won't see the tilt of his racquet head. If your motive is to get even, you will be deflected from your actual task. If you are dwelling on the event, you may not even remember which side to serve from. If, on top of that, you are feeling guilt for your anger, because the situation wasn't clear, then you not only have both emotions and their effects to contend with, you have the added unconscious intent associated with guilt, that of paying back for your crime. That's not likely to do you much good in competition either. Anger and guilt also will be discussed in some detail in the next chapter.

Here is an example of a slightly different type: One favorite opponent I have, who's certainly not the "psyching" kind, in that most of what he does is quite fair, has nevertheless the disturbing habit of raising his left hand slightly—sometimes only a finger or two—as he's about to return serve. It affords him some sort of balance, or enables him to line up his shot with a greater degree of accuracy. In fact, the technique of raising a finger at the ball is recommended for certain shots, like the overhead, as a way of guiding the eye or lining it up or improving one's timing. But in the game at sub-Wimbledon levels, in which one acts as his own referee, the raised finger signifies the opponent's shot is out. Thus, to see that finger each time one serves produces a slight hesitation, especially if the intention were to follow that serve to the net.

Now I have every reason to believe that my opponent is not doing it deliberately to throw me off. He is always quite contrite when I point it out, and encourages my notifying him as the only way to break him of an admittedly bad habit. Yet, despite the other's good intentions, I would still be at a disadvantage were I to let him get away with it. Thus, one can be exploited, that is, put at a disadvantage, without the other's being an exploiter, that is, without his seeking an advantage. This distinction is a further example of the difference between seeking an advantage and seeking to remove a disadvantage, between being offensive and being defensive.

In a way, this example is too formidable, because there is no denying the distraction that my opponent produces. In other examples, the displays are more subtle, resulting in both the disadvantage and a difficulty in calling attention to it. One takes time: before starting play, between serves, between receiving of serves, between games, before arriving at the court. One manages his equipment—adjusts headbands, towels a racquet, retrieves a ball. One calls his opponent's shots "out," or, at a higher level of play, observes their being called out. One talks, moves, and looks at his opponent—each a way of expressing some feeling, each a potential communication to the opposition, each a possible source of domination or submission. At least in chess your opponent sits at a different angle from your gaze than the playing field. Theoretically, you could avoid seeing anything of him but his fingertips.

TIME

In tennis, time is unfixed. A match can last anywhere from half an hour to five hours. You don't have fifteen-minute quarters. Baseball is somewhat similar in that respect, but even there, a game will generally last two and a quarter hours, give or take forty minutes. It follows that the use of time, in tennis, is largely up to the players. And that affords room for interpersonal dynamics to operate.

When you show up for a match is the first thing to consider, and since it is the first, if hidden, expression of anything between two opponents, it is potentially of psychological importance. I am speaking of a prearranged match. At the extreme, the manipulation is easy to recognize. Keeping an opponent waiting, by being inordinately late, is indeed exploitative—so much so that, in the big time, there are rules about it, pertaining to forfeiture. But one can be so intimidated by the thought of not being late that he feels he has to show up half a day early. (In psychoanalytic parlance, being very early marks you as an "anxious" type. But don't worry, you're caught, whatever you do. If you're habitually late, you're "hostile"; if you're always on time, you're "compulsive"; and if you don't show up at all, you're "schizophrenic.") Propelled by anxiety, the perpetual early bird's habit now has the side effect of engendering greater anxiety as he sits around waiting for the match to begin. One friend commented to me once that she was always anxious when she began play, and couldn't understand why. Having noticed that she generally arrived at the court about five minutes late, I asked her when that habit originated and she confessed that she got terribly nervous waiting around for a match to begin, so she always planned not to be early. The result—always being late—was no solution, since it became apparent that she was sure to be rushing to the match and couldn't help wondering whether her opponent would have found someone else.

Between the extremes, find your own best arrangement, but find one. My procedure has always been to arrive not more than five minutes before the scheduled beginning. Save yourself both the anxiety of a long wait and that of wondering whether you'll be late. Confirming this as the best policy for me is the fact that I notice that I'm most bothered when the opponent arrives specifically at that time also—as if he had no worries. And if I've been wondering whether he's going to show up at all, that also can work to his advantage, since the slight inclination to believe maybe I won't have to play at all to win this one gets dashed when he appears.

There is something of an old adage not to arrive first and be the one waiting, but I think it works only up to a point. Beyond that, as with my friend, one may have to worry about whether they'll allow you to play and, additionally, the opponent may recognize that you're groping. Muhammad Ali and Jimmy Connors may be able to march in when they please, but that's what happens when you have a television audience of millions that isn't about to tolerate the referee's forfeiting the champ because he wasn't on time. Don't emulate the stars, if you're not a star, because they can and do get away with more.

The warm-up period provides the second occasion for dominance, with respect to time, to be established. How long does it last? Who decides when it's over? How much time do you give yourself for certain shots and how much do you give your opponent? In professional play, there are rules, but in everyday play, there aren't. Or if there are, they are loose.

The one who decides it's over establishes control. He also puts the added burden on you of revealing that you need more practice. Don't make the mistake of fighting for the first by giving up the second. Take what you need.

Be sure to do this with specific shots that you practice during the warm-up period. For many, the only occasion on which they hit volleys is when they come to the net to retrieve a ball and decide to stay there. While this opportunity needn't be infrequent, depending on the ratio of overhit to underhit balls in your neck of the woods, it still may not be as frequent as you like, because you refrain from taking the time to come back to the net from the baseline. It looks like an imposition.

Especially for an amateur, one of the consequences of this reluctance is the obvious one that you're not getting the practice you need. It takes a good deal of time to hit a shot consistently. A few more forehand volleys could make all the difference between having the shot ready and never having it ready, since you can't depend on the match itself to provide enough opportunities to continue your practice with it. And the difference in the readiness of that one shot can affect other shots, other strategies, and your opponent's reaction to them. Like in a chess game, one good or bad move reorders what has happened and what may follow. The most careful artistry can be undone by a blunder, and a clumsy beginning can be immeasurably strengthened by one strong move. So go back to the net, even if it takes a few seconds, if you're not yet volleying as well as you can. And stay there, even after you miss, even after that great tendency arises to get out of there before you show him you can miss some more. If you don't miss them now, you'll assuredly miss them later at greater cost.

Then why is such a simple thing so difficult for so many of us? As already implied, because of consciousness of the opponent. You don't want him to think you're taking unnecessary advantage. So you give away your right. Would he like to practice the volley himself, and are you therefore usurping his volleying time? And what if you're missing, which is just when you need to stay there? Then he's not getting much out of it, since you're not getting them back to him to practice his passing shots. What image are you conveying about your game? Taking all that time to work on one simple volley? Will he note how really weak it is? Aren't you then refraining from practicing it in the rather forlorn hope that if you don't show him it's not there, he won't ever discover its absence? In the long run, that's bound to be a less productive procedure than trying to get it there. In the effort to construct the proper image, you avoid bolstering the reality.

The result, then, is the familiar pattern that I want to emphasize. You do get "psyched out"—by yourself, but there are many opportunities for the opponent to contribute his part—and you give up something that is yours: the time it takes to get a shot ready. Insisting that a person stand at the opposite baseline for half an hour while you work on your backhand top-spin volley, which either goes for a superb winner or misses completely, is a bit excessive. But are you therefore not taking the number of serves you need because you think you've got no right to keep him waiting? Or are you afraid to ask for too many overheads? Or any? Or any after you've missed one? How often does it happen in the match that the first overhead we approach we do so completely tentatively because the first one we hit in practice we hit off the wood and the second one we never took?

There are other opportunities along the temporal dimension for gaining, seeking, and resisting advantage. Some of the more obvious ones are the time it takes to change sides of the court, the time between serves, and the time between points. The general principle, however, is quite the same. Take what you need and don't worry about the opponent. As soon as you start being afraid that he's thinking you're taking too much or too little time, you get trapped in the image-saving syndrome again. It is likely to cost you your reality.

The exception is when you are in violation or close to violation of a real rule, and these exist only in the extreme. If you're taking five minutes to change sides, or serving your second ball before he's had a chance to return to his position of readiness, or swatting flies continually before he can serve his second ball, or bouncing the ball fourteen times after you lose a point, you're doing more than taking what you need.

This principle is important even when you think the opponent is taking unfair advantage. Don't spend all your time making a point of his unfairness, or you will have escaped his control only by yielding to his control. If you insist on moving away from the baseline to stop him from taking too much time, you will succeed only in giving him more time as well as control. If it allows you the opportunity of doing what you wanted to do—like toweling off your racquet—fine; but make sure the criterion of your choice is yours. Instead of making the point that he can't do this to you, make sure you take what you need when the time comes (which you should do anyway, but this way those more susceptible to guilt will have an easier time of it).

THE APPEARANCE OF THE OPPONENT

As a kid, I used to play a lot of ping-pong, and despite having become fairly good at it, I never graduated to the point of being able to call it "table tennis." My retardation, I am sure, was a form of reverse snobbery about being fancy. Nothing summoned up the competitive spirit as much as the well-decked-out opponent, who arrived with his racquet (which he referred to as a "bat") in a zippered case (leather, no doubt) and took it out to reveal that it was sponge on one side and rubber on the other (for a top-spin forehand and an under-spin backhand). In the face of such an entrance, I would deliberately locate the oldest piece of wood in the racquet box and take him on. Unable to gain the advantage with the finest and best, I would seek it with the apparent worst.

One of the best nonprofessional tennis players I know, a reputed heir to a two-million-dollar fortune, always arrives at the courts in an old raincoat, whatever the weather, looking like a retired "flasher." He carries his equipment in a dilapidated suitcase. He's short, pudgy, and balding, to complete the image. Not only is he the former City Parks champion, but he still, in his mid-forties, manages to cling to a top spot in any tournament. And as unassuming as he appears, he's as tenacious in not letting himself be undone in the match.

Is he deliberately "psyching" people out? Who knows? Maybe originally he was defending himself against the pretentious, as I was with my quest for an old piece of plaster or wood, but I'm sure by now it's as much a part of his tennis character as his drop shot. He would feel quite uncomfortable in a well-tailored, nylon warm-up suit, complete with matching underwear. But if his opponent manages to get exploited by his appearance, that's not my friend's problem. For if the opponent looked carefully, he would find that he never skimped on anything important. His sneakers (excuse me, tennis shoes) may not have had multicolored, parallel stripes on each side, but they were not the inexpensive variety that let your soles be pounded or your toes be cramped or your ankles be easily turned. In fact, probably one of the reasons I never advanced in ping-pong beyond the good-college-player level was not that I refused to call the game by its fancier name, but that I still liked playing with wood when the world of top players had advanced through rubber to sponge, to rubber on one side and sponge on the other.

"Appearance" can refer even to that intangible concept, "image." Roscoe Tanner, in the WCT tournament mentioned in the last chapter, was being heralded as "the new Tanner." There was even a reasonable explanation: Normally hitting a flat shot, he had been instructed in the advantages of top spin, so that there is more latitude (longitude, actually) for the ball to clear the net. Furthermore, he had ably beaten Borg early on in the tournament, a Borg who was playing well. Tanner was reputed to be aiming for nothing less than No. 1 in the world. As he had one of the better serves in the game, this did not seem unrealistic, especially with the addition of better ground strokes.

Was Tanner trying to "psych" out everyone else? I think the image he was trying to create provided an opportunity to free himself of being "psyched." Although he occasionally had scored victories in big events over the top players (Connors at Wimbledon in 1976, for example), he was still firmly ensconced in the second tier of the world's best, anywhere from No. 7 to No. 15, depending on the computer's latest quotations. The creation of a new appearance was an opportunity for others to believe that the victory over Borg was not an accident, as was the explanation of his improved technique. As a result, Tanner himself would not have to think, were he ahead in the match against someone reputedly better, that his lead was an accident. The opportunity to free himself from past manipulations was now present. Not a new "psych," but the removal of an old one.

BODY CONTORTIONS AND OTHER MOVEMENTS

Another favorite opponent of mine is the exerciser, the fellow who does a few neck twists or back arches, especially after he misses. "Ahh, if only I had time to practice enough, to iron out these kinks, how I could play the sort of game I'm capable of," is his body message. One of his cousins is the sufferer, the one who but for his tenacity in the face of a world dedicated to burying him as soon as possible would clearly be home taking care of his ailing body. With the slightest tinge of pain on his face, he crooks his elbow, turns it, and examines it, as if only he and his orthopedist knew the extent of his ailment and his courage in bearing it. Another is the equipment-checker, the one who repeatedly lifts up the sole of one of his shoes after he's missed, generally when he's been caught on the wrong foot and tripped over himself, or always runs for a towel or some sawdust following a missed volley, to try to correct his obviously worn-away grip. Sometimes it is the court's equipment that is obviously responsible for his poor showing, so he's continually returning to the middle of the net to make sure, by the racquet-and-a-half method, that it's either too high or too low.

Should one argue that there are plenty of rational reasons for this kind of behavior, and they have nothing to do with influencing the opponent, it could be disputed by pointing up the rather special occasions on which they occur. Nets are sometimes too high, sneakers do get holes in them, grips and elbows wear away, but why is it that one is so much more likely to notice these handicaps after a lost point? Could it be that in indicating the extent of his privation, the body contortionist can expect that those made aware of it would feel themselves curs should they exploit it?

STARING

"I knew I didn't want to look at her," said Evert of King, after their Wimbledon semifinal match of 1978. It happens in lots of sports. Boxers and opposing linesmen glare at each other. Batters and umpires stand toe-to-toe. But tennis has more variety than a simple stare of defiance.

There is, first of all, the stare to question the other's line call, complete with subtle implication that if he is willing to have it affect him, to begin thinking there was more to his last call than met his eye, then you certainly are not going to interfere with his reflective processes. It also lets him know that you are not about to make too much of it unless he volunteers, since you are a fair-minded person who respects his judgment (to say nothing of your inability to do anything about it since the call is up to him). It is, like other stares—the one at the cashier who's given you a dollar less change than you deserve, or at the person in front of you who's let the door slam in your face, or at the child who's just thrown his bottle out the window—designed to let the other know that he's made an egregious error, which, even though you may not have the resources to undo, you are still permitting him to atone for, if not now, at the first available opportunity.

On at least two occasions where such a judgment of mine was subtly questioned, I threw in the towel not only on that call, but apparently and unconsciously, on the subsequent part of the match. I assume that is what happened, since the tide changed completely in my opponent's direction following his stare at my line call. In both cases, I had been sure of my call. In one, I called his first serve out, and when I got that stare, asked him if he thought it was in. He replied that he thought it had hit "the outer edge" of the line. I was ahead 3–0 at the time, and so intimidated was I by the suggestion that I had gained something to which I was unentitled, I not only gave him the chance to do it again, but gave him the point. If it had been in, I reasoned, it was his point, since I couldn't have reached it. He went on to win the set, 7–6. In the second instance, I turned to some spectators to ask their opinion, when my opponent stared at my line call. One, who had been sitting almost directly in back of the line, volunteered that he thought it was just in. I gave my opponent the point, and from 0–2, 0–40, he went on to win 6–3.

The explanation is relatively simple. Giving up your right to your perceptions is giving up a lot of control. If you were leading, you must now imagine that it was because of —or could be interpreted as being because of—error. And there's no better way of getting one's opponent to engage in such reflection than by that inquisitive stare.

Aside from not being intimidated enough to change your line calls, how do you appropriately react to the glare of the opponent who has stopped in his tracks with a "you-called-that-out?" look at you. If you hold up your hands a quarter of a mile apart to indicate to him that there's no question about it, it's as bad as doing what I did, mumbling some combination of oh-did-you-see-that?-I-thought-it-was-out-you-want-to-take-two?-no-its-your-point. On the one hand, you're exaggerating in his favor and on the other, in your own. In both instances, you've allowed his questioning stare to have too much effect. The only appropriate response is to say, in a clear but modulated voice, perhaps with a half-an-inch nod (or better still, an eyebrow nod, with no head movement), "yup." This response conveys what it is designed to—I made the call, it was correct, I'm confident it was correct—and thus nullifies any effect the stare might otherwise have.

There are a couple of other important stares. One is used to follow your winner past the court until it comes to rest, especially at a critical time. It announces that there was nothing accidental about the shot. It has the flavor of "rubbing it in," but, again, it's important to recognize the distinction between being offensive and defensive. If you stare at your opponent on such an occasion, you're rubbing it in, especially if there's a curled-lip smirk added to it. (Connors is often guilty of that smirk and probably knows it, since he often walks around with a smirk. This doubtless makes it look natural and so covers up the occasions when it's deliberately humiliating—like after he's hit a winner off the opponent's winner.) But the stare itself needn't be humiliating. Its intent is to remind the opponent to think twice before doing that again. It is quite appropriate not only when you have hit a strong winner, but when you've hit one off your opponent's attempt to be clever—like a lob or a drop shot. It says I outsmarted you when you tried to outsmart me, and if you're likely to think this augurs of the future, I'm going to give you every opportunity to think just that. It is a defiant stare, worn when you have returned from the brink, saved something, and emphatically made your point against all opposition. So there! it says, quite defensively, in contrast to the grinning, offensive "Whom-are-you-kidding?" stare.

There are others. The stare at the ball that whizzes by you so fast, particularly on the serve, that it's important not to be looking at your opponent and be affected by any of his stares (either because you called it out, or because he's staring at the referee). In addition, you don't want to convey the impression that the call was in any way affected by your inability to reach it. It's a return-to-your-previous-position stare, an occasion to regain an instant of time, a more secure position, and a modicum of confidence. It's a stare away from rather than at your opponent.

A minor variety is the stare at the heavens. Unbelievable! Heaven help me! It's a bit dramatic and likely to be overdone, and can sometimes be replaced with a deep sigh or a subtle immobility. It usually occurs on such occasions as the opponent's hitting his third let-ball in a row. The particular message conveyed by each type of stare is most in evidence here, for anyone can see how inappropriate it would be to stare upward when your opponent hits a winner. If you're telling the world that your opponent's strength is unbelievable, then you don't have much chance left. In fact, the only occasion on which you are likely to witness this heaven-stare in response to an opponent's proficiency is when one player already considers himself out of the match and is shaking his head and staring upward in disbelief as a form of congratulations to the opponent.

It follows that the best defensive policy is to be as inscrutable as possible, if you do not wish to be unduly influencing your opponent or unduly influenced by him. It probably is the only way of not being guilty of infractions and not suffering guilt with respect to them, of neither manipulating nor being victimized. This lack of demonstrative response to the other's behavior may also serve to keep you calm. Should one argue that this kind of control necessarily would produce explosions off the court, one would be in good psychoanalytic company. There are others who contend the opposite, however—that control can become a habit. Luckily, however, behavior off the court isn't nearly as important as behavior on, so we don't have to resolve the issue.

TALKING

Some people talk more than others. The tennis court seems to be as appropriate a place as any for making that observation. Quite aside from the personality differences which distinguish those who value talk from those who don't (in Freudian theory, the "oral" type seeks any kind of gratification associated with the mouth), our everyday language implies something of the repute in which talking is generally held. "Talk is cheap," he's a "big talker," he's "all talk," "big mouth," and—it must be Australian—"motor mouth," as I once heard Rod Laver call a particularly voluble Ilie Nastase. These descriptions refer to the power of talk itself, its significance in hiding or disguising other things (like "actions"), and the effect it may have on the one who listens. Talk can be a weapon, especially in competitive situations. If you brandish it, it will be to your advantage to understand when it is offensive, and whether you intend it to be.

The extreme is again evident. As extremes always are. You don't chat away at your opponent in the course of a point. Not if you're playing a match, that is. But short of the extreme, there is ample room for maneuvering and resisting maneuvering.

Although players don't talk very much during points, there are enough interruptions in play to provide plenty of other occasions. Between points, between games, between changes of side, especially. Some do it, I am convinced, as an active form of manipulation, whether they're conscious of it or not. Others don't, but it often has that effect anyway (like the player who always announces the score between points, but only when he is winning). Invariably, I feel victimized by court talk, and I never initiate it, for, whichever way the match is flowing, talk can have a profound effect.

It is not simply that talk is distracting. When I'm behind in the match and the opponent is continually chatting to me or the spectators about irrelevant matters, I can't help thinking that he is deliberately trying to prevent a comeback, as if his air of informality were an assurance that he hadn't a care in the world. Or worse, his comments about how hot or windy it is seem especially solicitous— as if, by implying conditions are not quite right, he were subtly giving you the excuse for failing, and asserting his dominance. Obviously, they aren't so horrendous as to be applicable to his performance. The opponent who's behind, on the other hand, who tells you you're really playing well today (as opposed to every other day?), I can't help feeling is trying to undo your advantage.

At some point, I would like to develop the appropriate response to each of these provocations, but certainly not in the middle of a match. Like the response to the rhetorical question, "You called that in?" stated or implied by the opponent's stare, the only possible way to avoid getting trapped is to accentuate brevity and inscrutability. The most modest of smiles, generally with an ambiguous turn to them, is my only manner of defense.

In a match in the 1977 U.S. Open between Billie Jean King and Kerry Melville Reid, one that received some publicity because King lost her temper, talk played a critical role. The match had had a particularly dramatic buildup. King, engaged in a "comeback" after having been No. 1 for a long time and then retiring, was beginning to show signs of strength for the first time and to move into the top ten. Reid, always somewhat known but never a presence at the very top of the rankings, was moving up —a result, apparently, of having played much team tennis the previous year. Setting the stage further, Reid lost the first set handily, then came back to win the second. Was the first set mere nervousness on the part of the up-and-coming player? Was the second set "overconfidence" on the part of King? These are the questions that occurred to the spectator and enhanced the drama. Heightening it even further, the third set was neck-and-neck.

Then it happened. A conflict and some talk. King got mad over her error and knocked a ball into the stands. Reid said something to the referee. King talked to Reid during the changeover, Reid did not respond, and King went on to win the match in a tie-breaker.

King told reporters that what disturbed her was not that Reid had apparently asked for a "penalty point"—in fact, this request was her prerogative, since the U.S. Tennis Association, for the first time in this tournament, had introduced the concept to halt just such fits of temper as

King had displayed—but that when King asked her if that was what she had done, Reid did not respond. There was "no way I was going to lose" after that lack of good grace on Reid's part, King claimed.

Were King as alert to grace, and hence to manipulation, as she implied, she might have better known, as events demonstrated, why there was no way she was then going to lose. For she had clearly put Reid into a difficult situation, and had done so by her *talk*—and again, not just because it was distracting. Or because it "upset her concentration," another common explanation. King's talk was a very clever way of regaining control once she had lost it by her fit of temper, and afforded Reid very little opportunity to respond. Had Reid admitted that she had requested the penalty, she would have been forced into the position of defending herself for what needed no defense (a point conceded by King, who acknowledged the request as her perfect right). That's giving up quite a bit. And had she not admitted it, she might have then felt a double pang of guilt—for both doing it and not acknowledging it. Even if Reid had not made the request, and had told the truth, she would still have seemed to be justifying her behavior to her opponent. In each case, power would have passed to King, the power that often emerges with the other's talk.

I think Reid tried the best she could by not responding, by being inscrutable, but I also think it one of those occasions on which proper defense must lean to a bit more offense. Perhaps she could have tried, "You think I should have [asked for the penalty]?" The problems that come with either response would then have passed back to King. (To say "yes" would be an admission that she behaved badly; to say "no" would imply she wanted to get away with something.) But the complete handbook on tennis repartee has not yet been written, so silence—even though it didn't work here for Reid—is still the best defense.

Especially at particular times during a match, talk can reframe the drama. It seems to be well known that a spectator, watching even a modest level of play, ought not to interrupt participants to ask them the score. But what does "interrupt" mean, particularly in the informal club or park atmospheres in which many of us play? "After all, I waited until they were changing sides to ask," one might claim. "That's hardly an interruption."

Indeed it is. Aficionados may know that anytime during the match a request for the score from the players is an interruption, that if you're going to ask, ask someone who's watching and take your chances on the accuracy of the report. But is it known why it is so disturbing?

Even if it is the most informal match, and I know the inquisitor well, and I am merely sipping water at the net between games, I'll refuse to give out the score. And the reason, even though I may not always have known it, is that it changes things. There I am, having finally escaped the trend which put me down 3–0 at the beginning of the set, feeling a surge which accompanied my rebound to 3–2. To say "3–2" will be to negate that recent trend. (And if the trend were working in my opponent's favor, such negation, implied by revealing the score, would be potentially manipulative.) It would reframe the events I consider significant and make something else significant. And I fear it may have that effect on me, on him, on the game, on the drama. "But wait," I will want to say, "it was 3–0, but then I finally started coming to the net, and he started being indecisive, and then I stayed back at the baseline, and that's how I came back to 3–2, and that's what I feel I can continue." But I can't, not nearly in the same way, probably not at all, if I talk about it, because I can't say all that is really significant in my mind, and if I could I'd be telling my opponent an awful lot that I don't really have to.

What you say, when you say it, how often you say it, to whom you say it—are all potentially manipulative, even when the origin may be simply your own insecurity. I stopped playing with one opponent because, quite simply, he never stopped talking. Following each point, there was an obligatory comment. Not only "wow" or "nice shot," on those rare occasions when one of mine warranted it, but some extended apology to let me know that he hadn't played in a long time and that he hoped he wasn't taking up too much of my valuable time and "Boy, you can really put them wherever you want to." I used to feign tying a shoelace whenever balls were to be retrieved near both sides of the net, because I knew that from that face-to-face encounter, it was impossible to drag myself away before a good part of the hour was over.

Talking to spectators is manipulative. The professional who carries on conversations with the crowd in the grandstand is not simply "keeping loose." I often feel it's a ploy to keep the opponent at a disadvantage, as if the talker were removed from the immediate scene, as if he had some place better to be, or, if he's stuck with it, as if he had more to relate to than simply his opponent. It's like an opponent keeping track of the match on the next court. Whatsamatta? Aren't I good enough for you?

The simplest, seemingly most incidental remark can have a powerful effect. In a Rosewall-Connors match, discussed in Chapter 11 as an instance of how few good statistics are kept, one Connors comment did much to exemplify the offensive capability (in both senses) of speech. Rosewall had been playing well and offered some promise to his supporters against Connors, who had always dominated him. Connors had won the first set handily, but it was tied 2–2 in the second, with Rosewall seeming to have developed some counter-weapons against Connors' thrusts. Rosewall fell behind 15–40 on his serve in the fifth game and on the next point played well. He ran Connors off the court with a very deep and angled shot to the forehand. Connors just barely got it back, high, short, and directly over the center of the net. Rosewall was waiting. Just after he reached back and smashed it into the same forehand corner, Connors yelled out, "I can't chase *that one* down." The crowd laughed, Connors beamed, Rosewall (reluctantly) smiled, and Connors went on to win that game and all the rest.

The result may have been certain, considering the edge Connors had always maintained over Rosewall, but not its severity. Just as Rosewall may have been gaining some sense that he could come back in the match, just as he might have tied and gone on to win his own service game, after being down two game points and not having won his serve the entire first set, Connors aggressively and confidently conceded a point—after it was lost. Talk reordered the drama, restored control or power, diminished one player at the expense of the other.

That comment, I think, comes quite close to being unfair and manipulative. But it is a crowd pleaser, a seeming act of good will to one's opponent, a humble acknowledgment of an unreturnable shot (although, additionally, it is a direct comparison to Connors' previous accomplishment in "chasing down" the other one). These characteristics also make it extremely difficult for the opponent to respond. Can he say or imply that the other should shut up and play, without antagonizing the crowd, losing control, and making it obvious to the opponent that he's been strongly affected? Rosewall could do little but what he did, smile at the comment and lose.

I say it "comes close" to being manipulative, because the context in which it occurs must also be considered. Rosewall, Mr. Good Boy, had been using his own technique the whole match. As Connors revealed in mock imitation at one point, it was the famous Rosewall shuffle, characterized, after he misses a point, by walking slowly back to the baseline with eyes downcast and shoulders exaggeratedly hunched. But beware the opponent who gets too confident, thinking Rosewall has thrown in the towel, for like my raincoated friend described earlier in the chapter, he springs at you like a cat once the point begins.

So I can't fault Connors for the comment. Defense takes many forms. Connors, by the way, probably earned his Bad Boy image, like Bobby Fischer, from just such a refusal to be taken advantage of unfairly. Since the offense is often subtle, the overt response will usually be the one labeled "aggressive." (Perhaps part of Connors' reputed improvement in his image, of late, has occurred because his defenses have become appropriately more subtle.) I can recall one match when he ran across the clay court to erase the ball mark that his opponent, Corrado Barazzutti, was pointing at and asking the linesman to come over and examine. Nice guy, Barazzutti, underdog, rarely heard from before, and here it is, the U.S. Open semifinals, he's apparently getting bad calls, and his opponent doesn't even let him prove them. Right? Wrong. Who declared that this invitation to the linesman to come and get a second chance to make his call is fair? In fact, it's quite manipulative. It wouldn't be possible on other surfaces, and it's not always possible even on clay to see the entire, circular mark. It may even be the wrong one. Because of these difficulties, moreover, it is not an invitation extended by everyone or necessarily accepted by linesmen. It's a partial cure, at best, like having instant replay for some of the shots, but not all. Additionally, if the criteria of judgment change in the middle of play, one can never be certain what has produced the change. Is the linesman being intimidated? Is he anxious to show he's fair and in the process being unfair? Would Barazzutti have called him over if he thought

Connors' ball that had been called out was in? Beware of being offended by the obvious manipulations of the Bad Guy. They may be responses to the not-so-obvious ones of the Good Guy.

Most of us can recognize the feeling of annoyance or anger at an opponent who takes advantage of us. We don't like having to run after the balls he tosses to us, when we're always careful to deliver them to him at the right time and place. The thrust of this chapter has been to examine how often this kind of event occurs and what to do about it. The following are some further, summary suggestions:

1. If you're not ready to begin the match, don't begin. If you find that difficult, especially against someone who's ready to begin immediately, decide beforehand how long it takes you to get ready and stick to it (like twelve serves). If you're already feeling intimidated, offer your opponent some information, like the number you plan to take. If you get a grimace in return, ask him if that's all right with him. If he says "sure, sure," believe him.

2. If the opponent's in a real hurry, slow down moderately. If he changes sides without pausing, make sure you pause.

3. Never change a line call that you made in good faith. Never ask for a third opinion. Even if you "didn't see it." If you didn't, then you didn't see it out, so it's in. Giving yourself the benefit of some doubts takes its toll in guilt. Which leads to worse doubts.

4. Talk during a match only as a last resort against someone who's being actively manipulative. "Aha, thought you had me there!" accompanied by a pointed, waving finger, is about the worst I can think of.

5. Practice stopping play whenever a ball from another court rolls onto yours. Should your opponent then do it at

a critical time, you won't think it's particularly opportunistic.

6. When your opponent begins an elbow examination following a lost point, and you suspect malingering, ask him, without more than due concern, "Are you okay?" This will bring you at least one point beyond feeling sorry for his injury. He can still respond, with pain, "No, no, I'm fine," and exploit your charitableness some more, but that attempt can be dealt with by offering to stop and rest.

7. When you're losing, and you think you may have a chance, and you don't know quite what's been going on, but you have a distinct feeling you're being dominated, find some opportunity to express yourself that is not in response to what you imagine is the opponent's perception of you. Peel off a piece of your clothing, take two gulps of water, move to the other side without stopping—anything that is not specifically designed to impress anyone. Control and domination pass so easily from one to another of roughly the same ability that anything you can do to express yourself may regain something for you.

8. Arrive two minutes before your match is scheduled.

9. If all else fails, wear an old raincoat instead of a warm-up suit, and find a dilapidated suitcase for your paraphernalia.

CHAPTER 4

Emotions: Feelings Are Okay
If You Think About Them

"I was emotional," said Julius Erving . . .
"I felt like clapping, raising my fists, whatever, to get into the groove. We're going to
have to do it again and we're going to let our
emotions show. . . ."
"They can't sustain that kind of emotion,"
said Elvin Hayes.[1]

The Philadelphia 76ers didn't, it turned out, sustain it,
and went on to lose their Eastern Conference finals with
the Washington Bullets. It was, as the commentators were
fond of telling us, a highly emotional series.

The emotions have plagued psychologists for a century
or so, and as I once heard a leading psychologist remark,
we're always at the beginning in our study of them. But not
so limited, apparently, is everyone else. It is common now
to "get in touch" with our feelings, not to "bottle them up,"
to "express ourselves," to "stop intellectualizing," and to
be so "high" that we exceed all expectations. It is also common, unfortunately, to refer to being "blinded by emotion," or "ruled" by it, to such an extent that we may be
unable to "think straight" or perform at all. That leaves us
with a question that justifies the learned figure's reference
to our not having gone very far in our study of them. Do
they help or do they hinder? Particularly, performance.

[1] *The New York Times,* May 12, 1978, A17.

Particularly, competitive performance. Were Dr. J and the Big E assuming a commonplace, or did they have it backward?

One of the simple answers to the dilemma is that a certain amount of "arousal" seems necessary for performance, especially the competitive kind. Familiar to most introductory psychology students is the Yerkes and Dodson inverted U-curve, which, based on physiological measures of arousal, depicts performance as poor under both low and high conditions. Psychologists have therefore tended to draw the somewhat tepid conclusion that performance is abetted by moderate levels of emotion, not too much and not too little. This is consistent with the position of RET, discussed in Chapter 2, that emotional extremes do not work to our advantage. We need to replace the irrational thoughts with rational ones in order to overcome the debilitative effects of anger or jealousy or sorrow. This position would then indicate that a bit of excitement or being "up for the match" or getting "high" was ideal for yielding the best performance.

Part of the confusion is that we're not at all sure what emotions are, whether they're closely related to the "arousal" that physiological psychologists can measure in the adrenaline flows and heartbeats. About a hundred years ago, William James introduced the idea into psychology that particular emotional states were not dictated simply by a perception of an environmental condition—that they were not, in other words, beyond our control. "We do not tremble," said James, because we're afraid; "we feel . . . afraid because we tremble." [2] In fact, recent psychological experimentation has demonstrated that emotions seem to consist of what psychologists are fond of calling a strong "cognitive" component. It may be that you take note of the situation—

[2] William James. *Psychology: Briefer Course.* (New York: Collier Books, 1962), p. 377.

and then feel something that is more or less appropriate. Had it not been a lion that you happened upon, but an enticing maiden, then that quiver might have put you in a state not of "fear" but of "desire."

Where does all this put us? Emotions seem to affect performance, but we're not quite sure how. At least extremes, as suggested by the Yerkes-Dodson curve and RET, work against performance. At least thought, as suggested by James and RET, is influential in determining what we feel. And, finally, there is a strong case made by James that emotions "fit" the situation.

Rather than try to deal with *the* emotions, as a whole, and investigate their likely effects on performance, I have chosen to focus on the two I think are most controlling on the tennis court: anger and guilt. I am led to the conclusion that these two are responsible for much of what we do to ourselves, that they work against performance, that they can be controlled by thought, and that control ultimately rests in knowing when they're appropriate to the situation. Love, I'm afraid, counts for nothing at all in tennis.

ANGER

Finally, after Jeremy had been pushing her around all morning, grabbing all her toys, tugging at her overalls, drinking her apple juice, and pinning her to the rug with a body slam and a full nelson, Priscilla, two-thirds his size, a generally mild-mannered one-and-a-half-year-old, rarely averse to sharing her toys, always eager for her biweekly play group with her peers, even herself known on occasion to co-opt another's apple juice, had had enough. Sneaking up behind him, she put one hand on his overalls, another into his curls, and started yanking and shaking until Jeremy and his mommy, rushing in from the kitchen, begged for mercy.

Jeremy gets a little subtler as he gets older. And Priscilla's predicament gets more complex, her feelings of victimization more diffuse. Eventually, she goes into therapy to try to figure out why she's depressed so much of the time. And when she comes out, she's learned that she's been concealing her anger all this time, that she hasn't stuck up for her rights, directly, since she was one and a half. She takes up tennis to have a "healthy workout," or to find an "outlet for her pent-up aggression," and soon discovers that tennis only looks different from life.

Finally, after her opponent has once again called her shot out when it was clearly in by at least six inches, has tossed her the second ball just as she has stooped for the first so it either hits her in the mouth or she has to walk back to the fence to retrieve it, has held up his hand for the fourth time as she was about to serve, allegedly to wait for a passer-by fifty feet away from the court to stop distracting him, but really, she knows, to give himself an extra three seconds to catch his breath after the last rally, and with a pseudo-apologetic pose has begged her forgiveness after his mishit overhead caught both the top of the net and the outside of the line, she has had enough. With an outburst as shocking to her as it is to her opponent, she hurtles the racquet into the fence and stomps off into the locker room, swearing to play this stupid game never again.

Anger, by definition, is extreme. Clearly we all can recognize situations like that described, when we are no longer quite in "control," and when feeling as we do, we might as well give up on our game or activity for the day as try to proceed. Were tennis a thoughtless activity, there would be no reason why the excesses of the opponent should prove so debilitating. But they do. Even if we don't walk off the court, we might as well. Attention, physical movements, and perception seem all "out of control."

There would be little more to say about it, other than don't play when angry, except for two factors. One is that there is some hope, some way of modulating the extremity.

And the second is that, especially for those of us who happen to notice continually the pose of our opponent when he's lucky, or the way he returns our ball to us, or that we're capable of playing a lot better but are not sure that we'll ever demonstrate it, we would be extremely limited if we had to stop play whenever we got angry.

Consider, first, how often anger "fits" the situation. Someone runs into you as you step off a bus and almost knocks you to the sidewalk. You whirl around, ready to vent your spleen, and discover your assailant is blind and offering profuse apologies. Your anger disappears and you're ready even to offer assistance to him.

What has caused the anger that it could so rapidly disappear when you discover who is responsible? The injury? The humiliation? The blocking of a goal you wanted to achieve? Clearly not, when each of these conditions remains and your anger does not. Your anger depends on the degree to which the provocation is willful, or reckless, or, perhaps, grossly negligent. When the incident is demonstrated to be an uncontrollable accident, the anger disappears.

Thus, in the same manner that the punishment meted out by the law is generally in direct proportion to the degree of intent exercised by the assailant—premeditated malice is more punishable than recklessness, which is more punishable than negligence—so anger seems proportionate not to the injury we suffer, but to the degree of responsibility we place upon the provocateur. In that sense, in running parallel to our approximation of a system of justice—the law—the expression of anger is not unbridled, or uncontrollable, but very "fitting." In those cases where we find a person *should not have* acted that way, our anger is severe, compared to those in which we find the person less responsible for the effects of his action.

As discussed in Chapter 2, Rational Psychotherapists believe in reducing all emotional upset by substituting a new belief for the one causing the trouble. Since anger is debilitating, and caused by the determination that others "should not" act a certain way, RET therapists conclude that all "shoulds" are fabrications or simple extensions of personal preference. (Why *shouldn't* he knock into you? That's just your idea of what people shouldn't do.) RET therapists thus believe that all anger is inappropriate, and try to reduce it by getting rid of the person's "shoulds." This is generally done by replacing them with some such more rational belief as "It would be nicer if people watched where they were going."

Since the effects of anger are rarely positive, the attempt to get rid of it is understandable. I cannot, however, agree with this value of Rational Psychotherapy that anger is never justified. Simply wanting it to be so (because of its ill effects) does not make it so. People should not rush headlong into other people on sidewalks (and even in automobiles), and that's not just my personal preference. They shouldn't because it's not fair. Because it will produce innocent victims unnecessarily. Because it can be prevented without undue inconvenience to the one who is rushing to catch his train. Therefore, even though anger doesn't necessarily do you any good, it is certainly justified on occasion, so much so that my corrective for its ill effects is a function of thought and perception: Discover when it is appropriate.

If your opponent is manipulating you in some way, serving his second ball before you're ready, talking inappropriately, or engaging in the variety of devices discussed in Chapter 3, then it is certainly appropriate to get angry and fight back. How to do that may not be immediately apparent, but surely the starting point is a recognition of your right to that feeling, rather than obliviousness to anything your opponent does because you can't control it.

And, most emphatically, the right comes not from nature or liberated "getting-in-touch-with-feelingness," [3] but from recognition of its appropriateness in certain situations.

If you have done something stupid, then anger at yourself is justified. If your opponent does something culpable (from malice to negligence), then anger at him is justified. But if you *merely* do something that doesn't work out right, like miss an easy shot, then anger is not justified. And if the opponent *merely* does something you'd rather he didn't, like walk to his side of the net to clear away a ball, or call time when a ball from another court intrudes—both perfectly within his rights—then anger is not justified.

If all of this sounds a bit dogmatic, it is intended to be. Nothing accounts for a loss in tennis so much as inappropriate anger, at either oneself or the opponent. Nothing will serve as less of a remedy than the advice that, since anger is never justified, you had better get rid of it. Thus, the importance of noting its appropriateness.

The reason that anger at yourself for missing a shot is inappropriate is very simple. It happens all the time. Even when they're easy. Even to the best. So much so that more than half the points, even in top professional games, are won through error rather than outright winners. So it is not true that you should *not* miss easy shots; you should miss them.

Justifiable anger at your own actions is less common, but here's an example. Your opponent has hit a short ball at the net and you rush in for it. Just as you're about to hit it down the line, he moves that way, you go the other way, and you miss. You are appropriately to blame for having done the wrong thing, for the following reason.

[3] There seems to be a constant psychological war between those contemporary therapists who argue that anger is never justified and the others who assert that everyone has a perfect right to anything they feel. (Both are wrong.)

Your opponent's best strategy, as with the overhead that he can't cover on both sides of the court, is to cover only one direction. He can't tell you which one too early by moving to that side, because then you'll hit it to the other side. So his best plan is to move just before you hit it. Your best strategy, therefore, if he does this, is to hit it in the direction from which he just moved. Ahh, but that changes things. His best strategy is now not to move, but to cover the direction he was covering to begin with. And so on. So much so that your best strategy, and one advocated by the professionals, is to hit it right at him, so that whichever side he's going to move to will not be covered. But then, of course, his best strategy will be to expect that. The one thing, therefore, to avoid doing is to change your mind when you're just about to hit it. With all this potential guessing and bluffing happening in an instant, the last-second change often produces an error. It is especially important not to change as a function of the opponent's moving at the last instant, since moving is just what he should do (at least, in most of the strategic forays described above), and just what should be expected. The correct procedure, therefore, is to decide which side to go to or whether to go down the middle, and stick to it. Always do that. Get angry at yourself if you forget that and change your mind at the last second. It's justified.

The reason that anger at your opponent for doing certain things is important to recognize is so you don't burn yourself up with it. Some ways of dealing with his unfair practices are discussed in Chapter 3. It may be difficult to follow Priscilla's lead and grab overalls and hair, but when all else fails, and your opponent is still tying his shoelaces for the twelfth time between points on your serve, you can certainly adapt the technique by walking to the net, shaking a finger at him, and shouting at him, *"Don't do that!"*

GUILT

Although some players are convinced there's more than one rallying strategy ("Are we hitting *to* one another or *away* from one another?" one often hears), I think most would agree that a good way of doing it is to hit the strongest shot you can that doesn't take advantage of the opponent's being pulled off the court. People do differ in their ability to put the ball where they want to and this may account for some of the confusion about strategies, but that's why there are all those "sorries" when you hit a winner to the open court that you meant to hit down the middle. As a result of the general policy, rallying can be very satisfying. It can require you to hit deep and consistently as well as place it well from side to side.

When it works, the rallying is probably the best place for witnessing the cooperative effects of competition. Each gains through the other's strength. Each succeeds when the other succeeds. I'm sure this is why many tennis players never wish or have the need to play games. They do better when they're encouraging and being encouraged by the opponent, rather than trying to outdo him. (Neurotic reasons for preferring this activity are discussed in Chapter 5, on masochism.) I have rallied quite successfully with players of very different ability, some of whom could have easily beaten me, 6–0, and to some of whom I could have done the same. Conversely, when it doesn't work, there is nothing more frustrating than ending up rallying with an opponent who refuses to take a step toward a ball beyond his reach, or who won't hit one that's six inches beyond the line, or who seems to be deliberately volleying out of your reach.

Since you are trying to do something for one another, rallying is an excellent occasion for seeing the effects of guilt. In order *not* to convey the impression of unduly taking advantage of another or of looking out only for one's own interest, many of us will go out of our way to put ourselves at a disadvantage. We don't ask for shots directly at our backhand volley, which is what we want; we don't stay to hit ten more overheads, which we know will do us some good; we don't make our lobs too good when the opponent's practicing his overhead, since we fear it will look like we're trying to take advantage.

I can recall only one opponent, over the years, who was able, when rallying, to refrain from hitting a ball between bounces. The situation sometimes arises when you have hesitated long enough so that you can neither move in to get the ball on one bounce nor move back to get it comfortably on two, so you're stuck with hitting a half-volley. But sometimes you know, just before you hit it, that you're slightly too close for even the half-volley, so that when you swing, your racquet's going to meet the ball exactly at the ground and result in a scraped racquet and a ball that goes over the fence or into somebody else's court. And most of us do just that, because if we just take our racquet back at the last instant and let it go by, we're going to feel guilty that it will appear as if we're objecting to an errant shot by our opponent. We especially don't want him to believe, without reason, that he has erred, since we've been building up this wonderful rallying rapport, which consists mainly of our being able to satisfy each other without making demands. If we have been specifically hitting lots of shots that were technically out but eminently playable, how can we suddenly draw our racquets back?

The significance of this minor example lies in the effects of guilt. You do an injury to your game, the racquet, your opponent, and yourself, as a result of being unable to express what *might be taken* as an objection. To prevent potential damage, you inflict more damage.

Tennis encourages the intrusion of guilt, because some

opponents are notoriously able to inflict it. The stare at your line call, the raised eyebrow, the ever-so-slight hesitation before the server returns to the baseline (conveying disbelief that the opponent has called the first serve out) are all techniques learned in "Guilt Provocation I," of the School of Continuing Martyrdom. Since tennis is the sport where refereeing is so essential, and since it is mostly done by the players themselves, guilt is further encouraged. (At the uppermost levels, it is the referees who get the stares, and don't think they are beyond feeling guilt or are not manipulated by those stares. Eventually, as we'll see with the players, the tendency to give something back is strong.)

It would be merely a curiosity if guilt affected play only during rallying and thus resulted in your not being so well warmed-up for play during matches. But it does much more than that. To feel guilty is to give the other a lot of power. In psychoanalytic terms, guilt comes from the superego, the internalization of omnipotent parents' prohibitions. You feel guilty because you tell yourself that you ought not to have done something to the other person. You will then tend to compensate for what you imagine you've done by paying back the other in some way. (The referee does it by giving you a break on the next close call.) Can anything be more devastating with someone you're playing *against*?

Note that in a fundamental way, guilt is the opposite of anger, but both are related to how people "should" behave. You get angry when others ought not to do something; you feel guilty when you have treated others in ways you feel you shouldn't have or that might be interpreted as ways you shouldn't have.

In Chapter 3, I described what occurred on two occasions, subsequent to my guilt over questioned line calls. Not only did I change them, but the matches significantly altered direction from those points on. I am convinced it was because of the compensatory quality of guilt, the need to pay back. One might well ask why it wasn't enough to give the opponents the point they were questioning rather than the rest of the match. It was for the same reason that made me give them the point gratuitously. I had to wonder whether they were thinking I was taking unfair advantage of them. They saw me call a shot out that they saw in. They must be wondering how long I have been doing that and will continue to do that. I'll show them that they have nothing to worry about. And indeed they didn't. That's a lot of power they were bequeathed as a result of one little stare.

Does it help to be made aware of the guilt that others or you, yourself, are inflicting upon you? Sometimes, but not always. For another aspect of guilt is that, if you do become aware of your feelings, it leads to resentment. Having given away power to another, you now resent his being more powerful. Who are you to make me feel guilty? The accused resents his judge, the trespasser his captor. What elevated you to such a throne of judgment? Have you never erred, or been unsure of a line call? And resentment often leads to anger. "Who do you think you are?" evolves into "I'll show you that you can't do that to me." As should be apparent by now, inappropriate anger won't do you much good either.

Cure, once again, in contrast to both the get-rid-of-debilitating-emotions-because-they-won't-do-you-any-good and the let-it-all-hang-out crowds, lies in recognizing the conditions of appropriateness. Guilt is only appropriate when you are guilty: that is, when you are in violation of some code—ethical, legal, social—that has jurisdiction over you. Indeed, one of the reasons why guilt rarely has any advantageous effects is because both those who feel it and those who don't, do and don't do so inappropriately. One of the perpetuating impulses for criminal behavior is that the violator feels no sense of guilt for what he does, but justifies it through reference to personal or social circumstances. And, as we've seen, what makes a player swing at a ball he should let go during the rally is his concern about making the other feel bad rather than his concern for the game. What could be more inappropriate?

Guilt because you called a close shot out when that is how you saw it is inappropriate. Guilt because you called a close shot out that a second later you realized was not out is appropriate. The solution in that circumstance is the solution in all. Do what is appropriate. When you are guilty, make amends. In this case, change your call. This is one of the few instances on the court when the feeling of guilt is appropriate; as a result, if you ignore the feeling and stick to your erroneous line call, you will suffer (unless you're a psychopath who never experiences guilt). The manner of suffering may vary, but the general tendency would be to give back the debt with interest. Many may recognize the feeling that they ought to stick by their call, even when they now feel it was erroneous, and are so bothered by it the rest of the match that they more than make up for what they have taken. It would be much less costly, and fair to yourself, simply to change the call, to return the goods taken.

Guilt because you would like to take at least ten serves before you start, but your opponent has only taken two, is inappropriate. Guilt because you need about 120 to work out the soreness in your shoulder is appropriate. Take the first 110 somewhere else.

Guilt because you've beaten someone who's really better than you is inappropriate. Were he "really better," you wouldn't have beaten him. Unless you cheated. Guilt because you've cheated is appropriate. Don't cheat.

Guilt because you've beaten someone who's really a nice guy is inappropriate. Guilt because you've beaten a man is inappropriate. Guilt because you're better than your doubles partner is inappropriate. Guilt because you're worse than your doubles partner is inappropriate. Guilt because you're not as good as the person you're hitting with and he must be so bored or generous to be taking this time with you is inappropriate. Guilt because you're obviously better than someone else and he must be feeling so insecure that you better try not to look so good is inappropriate. Guilt because you're beating your son is inappropriate. Guilt because you're beating your father is inappropriate. Some people are better tennis players than other people. If nobody could play with anybody better, nobody would ever play with anybody.

The cure for debilitating emotions consists of judging whether they're appropriate or not. I think it quite fitting that those who advocate getting in touch with feelings at all costs (like some of the "Naturalists," discussed in Chapter 1) find judging or being "judgmental" the worst sin. As a result, they are prevented from making the useful distinction between appropriate and inappropriate causes of self-criticism, anger, guilt, and fear. If they can convince you that in a world where continual rankings, "seeds," favorites, and score-keeping occur, nobody is really judging anybody else, then you can try their kind of therapy. But for those of us unable to concede such purity of intention, there is another source of solace, and that is that being ranked No. 7 in the local club's listings is not necessarily a judgment of our total worth on the open market. While some of us neurotics may feel it is a divine decision, rendering us so much less humanly capable than No. 6, such an interpretation ought not to be the basis of calling everyone equal in everything. If it does anything, the reluctance to make the judgment prevents useful corrections for discrepancies. If I know he's better than me, perhaps I can pay greater attention to what he's doing. If I know he's better and still plays with me, perhaps I can better appreciate what it is I do well that others, even when they're better, can gain from. If I can judge when my fear is appropriate (the opponent is younger and has more stamina) rather than inappropriate (I just missed a forehand into the net, so I'll probably miss the next one), I can adjust my strategy accordingly. (In the first instance, "hit out," to prevent a long match; in the second, try the same shot again so as not to get "tentative.")

Acknowledging appropriate emotions is freeing. Expressing inappropriate ones is debilitating. Learning to judge the difference is critical. As knowing when one of my shots is stupid permits me to recognize one that is clever, so determining reactions that are inappropriate allows judging when they are appropriate.

CHAPTER 5

Masochism: There's Less to Losing Than Meets the Eye

For the third time this week, I heard the loser walk off the court saying, "I guess I just don't want to win."

PHONY MASOCHISM

One of the significant effects of our having entered a "psychological" age is the amount of credence often given to elaborate, deep-rooted accounts of behavior. I'm referring not simply to the use of jargon, although there's quite enough of that. (My six-year-old nephew reports that he's "really anxious" about entering the first grade next year. Probably because he doesn't know how to "relate to" an "overly structured" environment. I'm sure he'll have his "mid-life crisis" before he's twelve.) The belief still continues to spread, usually among people who have had experience with therapy or among those who know many with such experience, that all difficulties must lie in some ancient conflict between parents and the resultant subtle messages conveyed to the sensitive child.

While Freud certainly deserves to be credited for having begun excavating the depths of the psyche, it would seem that many in his entourage are unable to take the simplest steps without a psychoanalytic compass.[1] I'm not sure

[1] It can be fun to subject the study of psychoanalysis to psychoanalytic treatment. The desire to uncover the deep truth is obviously a repressed voyeurism—a symbolic representation of a wish to uncover other things (in some analysts, it's not so repressed). It's also a residue of early genital exhibitionism. See what power I've got?

whether being aware that I feel "anxious" permits me to know myself or my origins better. But I do know that I never met as many sufferers of "angst" or "alienation" or "depression" as I did during my training in psychology. Indeed, one could tell when my colleagues changed mentors or therapists by the vicissitudes of their holy afflictions.

And I don't believe I was jealous, or had sensibilities that were much coarser, or was so much less in touch with myself, as much as I believed that the diseases from which my peers suffered were a pretentious escape from some of the rotten inevitabilities of life, especially young-adult life, especially graduate-school life. If nobody ever ran over to you at parties to inquire where you had been all her life, if it was tedious to pore over academic tomes when the writing was often terrible, the exam to be given on them capricious, and the content either too old or too new to take seriously, if you couldn't write term papers because it was becoming too obvious that the only person who might read them was a graduate assistant who, knowing as little about the subject matter as you did, had to inflate his ego by pretending to find important errors in your work, then it was no wonder you weren't exactly sure all the time what to do to get the fascinating women to love you or the erudite professors to acknowledge you. To conclude from all this rejection and potential rejection that your feeling of worthlessness was simply a product of "alienation" or a construction of your elaborately complicated psyche was to ignore the contribution of the outside world and how painfully you participated in it. Such a conclusion was like, "I guess I just don't want to win."

The terribly unsophisticated fact about many of us is that we do desperately want to win, but don't know how. The rationalization of masochism comes from not being able to accept that conclusion. Its appeal is that it invites others to pay us attention—if not because of our expertise, then by virtue of how complex and interesting we are. Its effects are that we underestimate the strength of the opposition or the difficulty of the situation and overestimate our abilities.

It is not so easy to win. We are not so poised at the threshold of victory as we sometimes think. Some common ways we deceive ourselves on the court follow:

1. "Easy" shots are not always so easy. The overhead smash you've just missed requires very careful preparation and timing. For those who know how to do it, it's potentially the most effective of shots. But your missing it, when it's not exactly something you've been systematically working on, doesn't mean you're out to destroy yourself. Tennis, since it looks easy, increases the likelihood of this erroneous interpretation.

2. The shot you "always make in practice" but miss in the game may not be the same shot. With your opponent at the net, you must hit a passing shot, rather than an ordinary ground stroke. It's probably the latter that you remember always making in practice. The passing shot, as is well known, must be hit quicker, sooner, and with greater accuracy than the ground stroke. The passing shot that you always make in practice is in response to your opponent's hitting deliberately to your strength (if he knows how to rally). He's not so kind during the match. Your memory of what you do in practice also tends to be selective. You don't recall as many balls that were over the baseline, many of which may have been returned by the opponent anyway. Rather than "folding under pressure," because you "really don't like yourself so much," you are participating in a sport in which practice is very different from the game.

3. Victory was not as within your grasp as you made out. There is a tendency to exaggerate the proximity to winning.

If the home team scores 15 runs in the bottom of the ninth to beat you, 15–14, that event is understandably disheartening. But to claim that you "blew it" because you were ahead, 5–3, in the first set, and then lost in three, is to ignore the complexity of the tennis scoring system and the fact that there is practically always a missed opportunity to point to. Except in a complete rout, a point here and there often means a game here and there, and a few of those turned around often turn around a set.

What makes the issue even more poignant is that I-guess-I-just-don't-want-to-win people are not only often wrong, but quite difficult to bear. They imply to all who would listen that their potential success was assured, but for this funny feeling they have about it. By wearing their humility on their warm-up suit, they display their grandiosity. They seek to convey an impression of generosity through having given away something that was never theirs.

HEALTHY MASOCHISM

When you're no longer at the level where you stand to benefit by playing with just anyone, you enter an arena that not only the most sensitive find potentially vulgar. The mating dances in the waiting areas of some tennis establishments probably have few parallels outside of orangutan colonies or East Side New York singles bars. Potential partners solicit, cajole, parry with, abandon, reunite with, dominate, lie to, fight over, and betray each other with evident passion. No wonder that some players never arrive without a partner already in hand and some others never with.

In competitive areas, there may be a lot to lose by moving up. Every jockey who doesn't go all out with his Class B-2 mare so he won't have to face the B-1's the following week knows that. Woody Allen once commented that the most striking difference between him in his earlier life as a shlemiel and him today as a world celebrity is that he fails with a better class of people now.

Some of us don't want to move up for this understandable reason: We may lose the partners we have now, and who knows what we'll gain instead? It's comfortable to stay the same, for those who don't feel themselves superior to their surroundings, even with all the shortcomings.

Thus, being secure enough where they are is often the background of those who honestly want to lose. Who wants to face tougher and better opposition all the time?—especially when you can only discover new partners through the humiliating experience, to many, of announcing that you're on the make or available to be made.

Other healthy masochists may be afraid to move up. They may feel that they will become too good for the partners they have now, who will feel rejected. Such a feeling would be evidence, to a clinician, of a projected fear of rejection. Afraid of being excluded, you are unable to exclude anyone else. What is noteworthy is that whether the origin is security or fear may not matter. Escaping your fears is also a healthy sign.

WISHY-WASHY MASOCHISM

The general advantage of getting better is getting even better. To many, that's its appeal. To others, that signifies its senselessness. And there is good reason for each view.

Two conflicting tendencies exist in nature and in man. The first is adherence to the law of parsimony, through which the simplest, most direct path to a goal is chosen. The infant makes no voluntary detours as she pursues her treasured object. The crow flies to its destination as "the crow flies." In Freudian theory, this tendency is biologically based and elaborated into a principle of tension reduction. We seek to reduce states of excitation. The release of orgasm and that of sleep are examples.

The opposite tendency is found in the law of mobility. The infant and the bird do seek to get somewhere, while they could have stayed where they were. Orgasm is achieved only after a state of excitement; indeed, it is a state of excitement. The urge to do something is in continual opposition to the need to reduce tension and rest. Life against Death.

If masochism refers to the motivated defeating of one's own purposes, how is it likely to be interpretable when those purposes themselves are in direct conflict? Is it masochistic not to want to get better, since striving is a natural principle? Or is it in accord with the law of parsimony? Is it masochistic to push ahead, in violation of the principle of tension reduction?

In a match with a weaker opponent, I once noticed myself deliberately playing to his strength rather than to his weakness, without having been aware that I was doing it. Is that masochistic? If you want to win the game, yes. It's clearly not the best chance, not the shortest path to that goal. If you want to get better, no. The easiest path is not the one that elevates performance. Thus, trying to win in the short run and trying to get better are distinguishable, and the latter may be what the seeming masochist is up to. My opponent had been continually overhitting with his forehand, and I started hitting everything to his backhand, the more consistent side. Apparently, I wanted longer rallies, without having been aware that I was doing anything but trying to win the point. I happened to have succeeded on both attempts. We played longer rallies and I won the majority of them. I easily could have failed and been accused of masochism.

"Not wanting to win" could be a refusal to accept anything that could easily be yours, or it could be a way of challenging the opponent's best, rather than taking a simpler, more parsimonious victory.

MASOCHISM AND IRONY

Winning and not winning are intimately connected. Oftentimes you want to win so badly that you lose. Ironically, had you not wanted it so much, you would have had a better chance of getting it. Indeed, therapy for this dilemma is immediate and contributes to the irony. Give it up, and you're more likely to get it.

In Chapter 2, one of the mechanisms that underlies "choking in the clutch"—thinking it would be so awful to fail—is discussed as a potential cause of failure. There are other psychological processes that may account for ironic failure. They are quite important to tennis, since "the pressure's getting to him," the "folding" at the worst moment, the getting "tentative" are such commonly described phenomena and imply failure for which we alone are responsible. Irony poses the question: How is it we manage to do specifically what we don't want? Masochism answers it prematurely: It must be that we really do want what we don't seem to want. A study of the psychological processes by which demand prevents attainment can help to explain why the masochistic explanation isn't sufficient to account for the ironic result.

You check the seat belt a dozen times to make sure it's securely fastened. Even while you're driving. Even as you crash. You want to be sure to have enough money with you. So you take out your wallet and count it all the time. Exposed that often, it becomes more vulnerable. The money gets lost or stolen. You want to have lots of friends. You seek everyone out. You agree with everyone. Eventually, your friends discover you're agreeing with everyone, including the ones they disagree with, and think you're a phony. So you lose friends.

You have a great need for security. So you try very hard

to attain it. You want to be sure that the things you have are solid, the relationships fundamentally sound. You subject them, therefore, to continual tests. You challenge people to see if they can meet your criteria of solidity. If you're not putting them to hard tests, you're putting them to many —and eventually they fail you. Either they're not perfect or the testing itself wore at their durability. If you weren't so insecure, they wouldn't be failing you, and you'd have more security.

Did you want to lose health, money, and friends? Hardly. You wanted them so much that you either risked their loss through your constant attention or else lost sight of the end, while you were concentrating so hard on the means.

You want to win. You know you're good enough. Near the end of the match, ahead 5–3, you miss an easy shot. You get furious with yourself. You sense you can't do anything right. The anger itself clouds your vision, makes you not notice what you're supposed to be noticing, makes you too impatient to wait for the proper moment. From your wanting to win so much, your opponent senses how far from it you are. He begins to be aware of what you do wrong, of how vulnerable you are.

Did you lose the match because you can't stand to win? Quite the opposite. You couldn't stand to lose. Your lead wasn't so insurmountable. The shot you did miss wasn't that easy or critical. But here, with victory close and so important, that failure assumes paramount importance. Like the blemish on the otherwise perfect face, it receives all the attention. Does it demonstrate that you want to find fault with yourself? No, it demonstrates that you want or need to be blemishless. You don't want to lose, you want to win —so much so, in fact, that you lose.

The effort spent in not making a mistake produces "tentativeness." You overhit, or miss a line, and focus on the error to such an extent that you become fearful of repeating it. You underhit, hit softly, hit down the middle, and are easily exposed to danger. So attentive are you to not erring that you err. Tentativeness recognized then produces its opposite. Having sensed that you're tightening up, not hitting as deeply, not following through, and getting worried that you'll suddenly miss, that you've lost a few consecutive points, you then try for extremely difficult shots. Rather than seeking to gain an advantage slowly, you try to hit a winner off a service return, or hit a line on every shot. The result is inevitable. Winners are not only harder to hit back, they're harder to hit. The former is what makes them winners, the latter what makes any sport interesting. Greater rewards for more significant accomplishments.

The smashed service return goes into the fence, you shake your head, can't seem to understand it, rationalize what you've been doing by telling yourself it's not your day, and hurry through the rest of the match so you can dash off the court. What is so oppressive? Winning? You haven't given it a thought. Being completely confused at this point about how to proceed, suffering because you've run the gamut from caution to risk and failed at both extremes, you can only hope to start over on another day, when the particular sequence—smell of success, greater attention to errors, tentativeness, and extreme risk—hasn't left you ultimately so desperate.

Interpersonal perceptions can add to ironic consequences. Becoming extremely distraught over your foolish mistake is partly an effort to prevent criticism from others—the opponent or the spectators. You hope to minimize its significance by doing your own ridiculing. Others, it would seem, can't help thinking you less of an idiot should you at least have the good sense to know you're an idiot.

The irony is that the opposite is true on the tennis court. Throwing the racquet, shaking your head and looking disgusted, far from improving your image in your opponent's eyes, lowers it. Not to realize that your mistake was quite common, or one you've made before, or one that was produced not by your lack of expertise but by his extremely clever, well-placed, top-spin lob, which, although somewhat short, nevertheless was placed just far enough toward the direction you just came from so as to catch you on the wrong foot, makes you more of an idiot. To walk back to where you came from, without the slightest sign of self-incrimination—now that would be impressive. He who makes unforced errors and knows not that he makes unforced errors is a fool. Teach him. He who makes unforced errors and knows that he makes unforced errors is a sage. Learn from him.

In some of the psychological literature on behavior and communication, a pattern is identified that helps systematize the process of irony.[2] The pattern is "complementary," in which as one person gets more his way, his partner gets more the opposite way. Examples abound.

He thinks she's too nosy and she thinks he's too secretive. To break through his secretiveness, she asks a lot of questions. This contributes to his feeling that she's nosy and as a result he clams up more. This contributes to her feeling that he's secretive. Both his and her efforts at cure contribute to the disease. To make her less nosy, he becomes more secretive, but this makes her more nosy. To make him less secretive, she becomes more nosy, but this makes him more secretive. Therapy is simple. Since she would have less need to be nosy were he less secretive, he can improve their relationship by becoming less, not more, of what he is. Since he would have less need to be secretive if she were less nosy, she can improve the relationship by becoming less of herself.

As he gets more pedantic, she gets more resentful. Her

[2] P. Watzlawick *et al. Pragmatics of Human Communication.* (New York: Norton, 1967.)

resentfulness makes him redouble his effort to make his point, causing more resentment.

As he gets more critical of her, she gets more in need of reassurance from him. Her greater need makes her expose more of her mistakes, in an effort to have them dismissed. The more mistakes he hears, the more critical he becomes. Were he less critical, she would minimize her need, and he would have less cause to be critical. Were she less likely to expose mistakes, he'd be less critical, and she'd have less of a need to be reassured.

R. D. Laing similarly describes such ironies.[3] Jack thinks Jill greedy because she wants more, so he gives less; Jill thinks Jack nasty because he gives less, so wants more. And, not to be sexist about it (Jack isn't the only one with something to give), Jack feels identically (i.e., that Jill is nasty because she gives less, so wants more). Therapy again consists of wanting what you want less.

By not accepting failure on the tennis court, or by calling it masochism, we contribute to it. Therapy is simple. Accept it, convey that acceptance, and one step toward producing it will be eliminated. Indeed, much more than one step. Nothing is so disarming to an opponent as showing you don't care about errors.

But beware! If you demonstrate, histrionically, how much you don't care, you will only contribute, ironically, to your defeat. Even the least psychologically sophisticated knows that when someone stomps and shrieks, "Who cares?" the answer is evident.

[3] R. D. Laing. *Knots.* (New York: Pantheon, 1970.)

CHAPTER 6

Avoiding Avoidance

For the fourth game of the 1977 playoffs with the Kansas City Royals, the Yankees, it was reported in the papers, kept their luggage in their rooms. This behavior was worthy of press comment, since teams that are down 2–1 in five-game series in the opponent's city invariably want to be ready to leave town as soon as possible should they lose. The point at which I became aware that tennis had more to it than bending the knees and following through was when I was about to serve in a game in which I was ahead 40–0 and my opponent walked back to the fence to throw me the third ball. Let them know you're not taking the luggage out early.

Many of the ways in which we lose in tennis reflect our seeking to avoid the knowledge that we're playing competitively. Absurd as it is, we deny—a favorite avoidance mechanism. What? Me, have a drinking problem? Go on, I just have a couple a day. Deny that we want to win, deny that we're trying hard, deny that we're actually playing in a match. To retrieve and throw the third ball to your opponent at 0–40, you have to admit that the game is still going on, that it hasn't ended yet, that it probably will end in his favor, but that it most certainly will if you try to hurry up and get it over with. How to make similar avoidance behavior difficult—like getting ready to leave town before you have to so as to avoid the embarrassment that sticking around will bring if you lose—is the goal of this chapter.

PRACTICE FOR REAL

Tennis is one of the few sports, if not the only one, which many participants find more enjoyable just "practicing." While other sports have warm-up periods, eventually they end and players get down to the real thing, the game. This is as true of schoolyard basketball as it is of professional hockey. You don't just practice your dribble and your jump shot, unless you're alone in your backyard (and even there, you might fantasize that an opponent is guarding you, or keep score, in some way, of the shots you're making). But in tennis, it would not be surprising to learn that at any moment more players were just "hitting" instead of "serving them up." Certainly, it was not until relatively recently that I started playing sets with any regularity, and I still will spend many hours just rallying with someone, not because I'm grooving my cross-court forehand by hitting fifty in a row without a miss, but because it's often more fun.

There are probably a few reasons why tennis has this distinction. One is that the game begins with a serve, and statistically it can be shown that the typical rally doesn't last more than three or four shots following the serve. Thus, the game is quite different from the rally, in which the serve is not usually used. Second, there is less action in the game and more walking around. You needn't wait, when rallying, for the opponent to get back to his position, for all the balls to be in place, for the next point when one shot is slightly outside the line. There's a lot more movement in rallying. And third, people generally hit much harder during rallying than they do in games, since they are not so restricted by the actual lines of demarcation, and since they are freer to try to improve without the risk of losing. Thus, except when players are really "match-tough" and have played an awful lot of them, the rallying is generally of a higher quality and more satisfying than actual match play.

Which is all the more reason for the principle. If you want to improve for match play, do not refrain from playing matches in practice, when the temptation is great to avoid them. Do not avoid creating as much as possible the actual conditions of match play. An exception occurs when two players are of quite different ability. They could still rally profitably, although a match would be no fun. This exception, however, is not nearly as frequent as is believed by people who argue it's better exercise just to rally. It may very well be just that, but I've seen many a match-avoider suddenly claim to be an exercise-addict.

Aside from the actual differences between match play and rallying, there are good psychological reasons for practicing under simulated match conditions. People do perform differently under different constraints and in different settings. The very act of participating in a psychological experiment (discussed in Chapter 10), for example, produces performance unlike that in the "real world." We expect different things from different situations, and thus we help produce them. Role-playing has become a popular technique in some therapeutic circles and has even been suggested as a fundamental alternative to experimentation in psychological research because of the problems of generalizing laboratory research to the real world. As graduate students, we were well advised to consider duplicating, as much as possible, actual conditions of examinations we were preparing to take. While few took the advice, those who wrote complete answers to hypothetical questions in blue booklets, within the appropriate time limits (and even, if they could manage it, in the rooms in which they were to take the exams), invariably reported that they profited from the experience.

Keep score. Play sets. Even when you're rallying, duplicate actual conditions of match play, if you're preparing for a match. I wouldn't advise never hitting an opponent's shot that's out, especially if you can reach it without much effort and swing at it without wrenching your back or crashing the fence behind you, but I would practice doing a few things that you simply might not be accustomed to doing enough of during actual match play. Like stopping when a ball from another court rolls onto yours during the middle of an exchange. Or like saying "Out," when a relatively close shot of your opponent's misses the line. The refusal to be so officious so as not to seem unduly petty or critical of your opponent when it doesn't count should be weighed against the possibility that you will continue to refrain from doing it, when you have close calls to make during a match (presuming, of course, it is of the you're-your-own-referee variety).

Don't avoid shots that you know come up during matches, but that can easily be ignored while rallying. Work on your volley. Go up to the net, even when you're not in the process of retrieving a ball, and stay there. Ask your opponent to hit shots only to your backhand volleying side for a while. Practice your serve, practice your overhead, practice your lob. Make up games to make it more difficult to avoid the things you'd rather avoid. Try hitting deep backhands to deep backhands in a 21-point game in which anything else but a shot into the rear box gives your opponent a point. Better to learn in practice how unprepared to do it you are.

BE ESPECIALLY ATTENTIVE
TO WHAT DOESN'T MATTER

Keep track. Of every drink you didn't have. If necessary, keep written records. If possible (it's slightly easier to do when you're out there), keep mental ones. Remember everything you can about what went on. Keep logs, schedules, diaries to assist you. I wouldn't be surprised if it's the acknowledgment of what's going on, rather than the group support, that gives Alcoholics Anonymous some success. You can no longer avoid it, deny it, minimize it, qualify it, or excuse it when you're bringing it up and talking about it in detail (you may still be able to rationalize it, project it, intellectualize it, sublimate it, and repress it, but at least you've moved on to more sophisticated defenses). Weighing every last bit of yourself and your cottage cheese is an inescapable way of attending to those details that you and your psyche, interested in defending you, would prefer to avoid. It's no accident that would-be weight-changers start out as weight-watchers.

Of what should you be keeping such careful track on the court? Of the score, for one thing. (It's remarkable how much more likely we are to forget it when we're losing.) Of how the sequence went during the last game. It's difficult when you haven't done it, so get started doing it, and you'll see it's relatively easy. Rehearse, at the beginning, if that helps you. The more you can keep track of, the better. Some of the reasons for this attention have to do with dictating particular strategies of risk-taking, discussed in Chapter 9, but the general purpose is simply to avoid avoiding things. 0–40 is 0–40. It's not a blur and let's get it over with and begin again. Recognizing that particular score is an important step toward recognizing that it's a mere three points from deuce.

The sequence in games, the sequence from the ad and deuce courts, and the sequence from the north and south sides may each tell you things. A simple matter like knowing you're one service break behind, rather than being blown out of the match at 4–1, is a significant detail that can only help. You might think that people who are at the level of holding serve four of five times wouldn't need that advice, but it's equally applicable to those who don't hold it four of five times. If, losing 1–4, you realize there's been only one service hold, and that by your opponent, then you may correctly conclude that only one hold on your part, while otherwise maintaining the pattern of breaks, will draw you even. The basketball team losing 3–1 in the playoffs knows that it is only one "home court break" down, doubtless the reason for their fondness for playing them "one at a time."

Keeping track in tennis is helpful for an even simpler reason. As mentioned in the first chapter, tennis has at least four important dimensions which vary systematically. You either serve or receive serve, with a first or second ball, from the deuce or ad court, on one side of the net or the other. In the interests of fairness, everything gets switched. First here, then there, first me, then you. And, of course, you must win by two points, so attentive is the game to the necessity of not ending the square-dance asymmetrically. Even the introduction of the tie-breaker hasn't violated that basic principle. Alternate serve, alternate sides, and if the set ever comes down to one point (as in a nine-point tie-breaker), try to give whatever advantage you can to the one receiving—choice of courts, and first serve.

This elaborately constructed symmetrical design is affirmation of the basic tennis principle of fairness. You must Even Things Out. To accomplish that, you must avoid the Odd, or have two of everything. In basketball, soccer, hockey, and football, you do switch sides of the field, but that is essentially all. Tennis not only has the four dimensions already mentioned, but when you add the options of hitting forehand and backhand, cross-court and down the line, to the forecourt or the backcourt, there become 128 (2^7) different conditions worth considering. It turns out it's the return of the second serve from the deuce court on the south side, on which you've been rushing the net off the forehand to hit cross-court, that's been doing you in. You should have been going down the line.

Did I say keeping track was a simple matter? No. No

wonder that not thinking is so seductive. There is too much to think about. But only if you need to be thinking about everything. The importance of this elicitation of tennis dimensions is that it reveals something critical: any one of them could be addressed systematically, but only if it were recognized as potentially capable of influence. I find it constructive, for example, to note the difference in games won from the north and south sides, because I once discovered that there was a much stronger relationship between that factor (or "independent variable," as it's known scientifically) and the winner of the game, than there was between server and winner. This relationship might only be more critical at the level where serves aren't so powerful, and on courts where wind tends to be a major factor, but I'm sure those two influences are not unique to my experience. Having discovered that relationship, and kept track of it, I was able to do something about it. I had noted that the tendency was to overhit with the wind at my back, and to play much more consistently from the downwind side, since against the wind you could hit as hard as you liked and it would stay in. Working from that principle, I began to make some headway, by rushing the net against the wind so as to encourage the overhitting of the opponent, and hitting with much less pace from the upwind side to gain some consistency. (This strategy was probably the opposite of what I would have been advised to do, had I known the wind difference, but not kept track of where games were being won.) I found, by being attentive to one of those seven dimensions, that a condition which frequently exists in everyday play was instrumental in determining the winner.

But what do you do about those manifold possibilities? Cognitive capacity is certainly not unlimited, especially under the conditions of play. Bearing in mind this chapter's title, however, what you do is use those various conditions to remind you of what's potentially important. The tendency is to avoid recognizing specifically what may be causing the trouble. When you can hardly help noticing something, like your volley isn't working, you avoid noticing it. By paying greater attention to which side it isn't working from and on what occasion, you have the opportunity to be more articulate in your conclusions. The pundits are right when they advise changing your game when something's not working. But which of those four or seven or 128 games you should change is often not immediately apparent.

NOT ONLY WHAT AND HOW
ARE CRITICAL, BUT WHEN

So you've really digested the avoidance lesson. You're determined to notice, to record, to face, to confront, to avoid avoiding. You're going to tell your boss, your lover, your colleague what you think, instead of pretending that all is bliss. You proceed to confront him with your insight, get into a fight, and make an enemy. You notice the events that you've been avoiding, that only from the deuce court are you winning with your volley, so you stop hitting it from the ad court and instead of losing in a close set, you lose in a romp. So much for avoiding avoidance.

Fundamental to the use of particular strategies, discussed in Chapter 11, is knowledge of critical occasions. Their being critical signals some direction in policy. Unless you know they're critical, the signal isn't there. You may be doing the right thing, but if it's not done at the right time, it may not matter.

The causes and effects of critical events are later discussed in relation to statistics. (As Chapter 11 outlines, events like "The Long Anything," "Lost Opportunities," "Returns from the Brink," and "Take That!" are highly significant, as can be determined by what happens subsequent to them.) The basic principle, presented at this point, is simple: Learn to Take Advantage of Critical Opportunities. The subsidiary principle is subtle. When you're at a loss how to get back in a match, try to create such opportunities.

Here is an example. There is some technical advantage to bouncing around on the baseline when you're receiving serve. It prevents your being "flatfooted," and gives you a head start on twisting the body. But there is great psychological advantage to doing it at the right moment. If it's a critical point for the opponent, it invites him to be distracted by it or consider it too seriously. It invites the opponent not to be in charge when he should be in charge. It asks him, if he's willing, to think of which side to serve to, since your step in one direction or the other dares him to look for a new opening. It asks him this at the last possible moment, when there is not enough time, generally, to alter his strategy. And if there is enough time for him, there's enough for you to move back to cover the opening. Like hitting a return of serve, in doubles, cross-court or down the line, or like "poaching" or not poaching, the occasional use of a sound strategy cannot only neutralize the other's potential advantage, but can do so at just the time he can least afford it.

The result of such moving, I have often noted, is that the opponent double-faults in a significant number of cases. He does it often enough, even on a professional level, on occasions identified as critical. By recognizing them, you, the opponent, encourage it even more. Should you consider it unfair to have this advantage, then give your opponent the same advice, or show him this chapter. Knowledge is always unfair if inequitably distributed. But if you think it is unfair manipulation, then you're not allowing yourself the full benefits of knowledge. Moving at the baseline is not only permissible, it's recommended. Unfair manipulation would be using those moments to bend down and tie your shoelace. (Note that a team can call "time out" just as the other team's kicker is about to attempt a field goal.) Or jumping up and down. (Note that a home-team crowd can jeer all they want when the other team goes to the foul line.) Or kicking the sod off your tennis shoes when the opponent is about to throw up his second serve. (Note that a batter can step out of the box as the pitcher begins his wind-up.) Compared to football, basketball, and baseball, tennis is the fairest of all in that recognition of critical moments permits behavior that is part of the game, rather than a distraction from it. The psychologically knowledge-able are thus distinguishable from the opportunists of the psyche, or, as Chapter 3 emphasized, giving yourself every advantage is quite distinct from seeking to give your opponent every disadvantage.

As emphasized in Chapter 9, the general strategy related to critical occasions consists of playing conservatively. If your opponent has just missed an easy shot, your "hitting out" will only give him the chance to recognize that you can err as well as he can. If the point is critical to you, exuberance only demonstrates a wish to get it over with as soon as possible. The time not to be a gambler is when there's a lot to be lost.

As suggested earlier, the subsidiary strategy, with regard to critical occasions, is to try and create them. If you need them, and they're not in the offing, you'll have to provide your own. Do something you wouldn't ordinarily do. Set the opponent up. Give him an overhead or drop shot. Allow him to miss. And if he doesn't miss, go for a winner off his winner. It is for extreme cases, where you are genuinely being dominated. Not only give yourself some chance, but a chance that has critical meaning. More details about what constitutes the critical event will be provided in Chapter 11.

Of course, the converse is also true. When you're way ahead, stay away from critical occasions. Don't try to accomplish anything of significance. Accomplishing things is for people who are behind.

YOU CAN ONLY DO SOMETHING THE FIRST TIME ONCE

Alas. It's just not the same when we revisit Paris or make our second million. Is it a fault of memory? Of perception? Of motivation? All that, at least. Good things become better in our recollection. The novel is seen differently than the familiar. We strive more for the remote than for that to which we're accustomed. But whatever the reason, we can be sure that the initial occasion is distinctive—more attractive or frightening or awesome. It may be why psychoanalysts make much of childhood, poets make much of first love, and Otto Rank makes much of a little thing like being born.

The lesson from this observation is really a meta-lesson, a lesson about lessons. When you're trying to learn a lesson, always give it more than one chance. There it is 0–40, he's serving, and remembering something from an early page of this chapter, you make a special point of walking back to the fence to retrieve the third ball, and toss it to your opponent. Let no one think the game is over. He promptly wins the next point and the game, and throws you all three balls back. You abandon this silly principle, all others, and take up a really thoughtful game like weight-lifting.

First of all, nothing works all the time. Willie Mays once dropped a fly ball (true, he was seven and a half at the time) and Jimmy Carter once took an unequivocal position on something. Second of all, things take time—especially things you want to change, and more especially things, like tossing a ball back, that are designed to have an influence on someone else. Third of all, the point of effecting a change in policy is to change the odds to being more in your favor than they had been, not necessarily to being more in your favor than in someone else's. Maybe your new résumé will now get you an interview in 1 out of 5 cases instead of 1 out of 500, your new charm will gain you acceptance in 50 percent instead of .05 percent of your attempts, and the change in your tennis strategy will enable you to win the 1 out of 3 games in which you are behind 0–40, rather than 1 out of 16. Those changes in the odds are decided improvements, but they do not imply that success will be yours all the time; in fact, according to those figures, it won't be yours most of the time.

But it's important to refer to the distinctive characteristics of the "first time." It is so different that it's the worst occasion from which to generalize. I am to this day convinced that my economic history would have proven substantially different had I not won the "daily double" the first time I placed a bet at the racetrack, and that the gods and the New York State Racing Authority "hustled" me. If we were all to base our ambitions on first-time successes, few ever would have made it to the tennis court, much less to the typewriter to pontificate about the tennis court. So, fourth of all, the first time, as exemplified earlier, is a time all its own. And fifth of all, the knowledge that the first time is distinctive puts a very different aura on the second time. And that requires a paragraph all its own.

I referred to the match in the Preface. The American Airlines semifinal, Raul Ramirez against Peter Fleming. Fleming is hardly the television personality that Ramirez is (the match is being broadcast on Sunday evening, prime time, network television), but he has been sizzling all week and is dominating in the match. It's the third set and Fleming hasn't had his serve broken since the first. He's a break ahead at 4–3 and serving. If he holds here, he's a game away from winning the match. On the first point of the eighth game, Ramirez does something different. He runs around his backhand on the fourth shot of the rally, the return of the volley, and hits it into the net.

It didn't work. It didn't work the first time. But it didn't have to, because the idea, in Fleming's head, that something new could emerge turned that match around. The idea that Ramirez could do something with points off Fleming's serves, the idea that he could seek to gain advantage over them, made Fleming aware of and afraid of the second time. A second time that never came. A second time that didn't have to.

It may sound absurd, but since this game hinges so much on what you think, and what you think the other's thinking, the effect of Ramirez' runaround can be understood. He appears to be up to something, he appears to be fighting for his rights, he appears to be thinking, and although he's netted that shot, he may have found out something. Wasn't Fleming bothered enough by these thoughts, consciously or not, to volley the next point into the net, and then double-fault three times in the remainder of the game to give Ramirez his first break of the set? Ramirez held serve, and then broke him again in the tenth and last game.

Ramirez had not, to the best of my recollection, tried running around his backhand at any point earlier in the match. It was even more noticeable because it hadn't previously occurred. And as it signaled something to the viewer, so it signaled enough to Fleming.

Additionally, Ramirez' maneuver was smart. Although his answer was incorrect—he did miss the shot—he presented evidence of his being thoughtful. (Notice how the word itself indicates less about the result than about the process.) When you know you've done something thoughtful, or not so thoughtful, or the opponent has been thoughtful, then the game shifts. In tennis, it is even more important than being strong. Strength can come to everyone, strength can come from desperation. The blistering return of serve is important, but not nearly as much as the receiver's shifting position, for the latter suggests, It's never over, I'm always going to be thinking of ways to win.

Even in matches where one player wins handily, shifts can be seen to occur in direct relationship to having been smart. Chris Evert was clearly the favorite in a recent encounter with fifteen-year-old Tracy Austin (semifinals, 1978 "Family Circle" Cup in South Carolina), but the match had provoked much interest. Austin was a lot less experienced, but had reached the top ten, and had the consistent game that just might give Evert trouble. Evert began by winning the first three games, including eight of the first nine points. In the fourth game, Evert came in on a relatively short ball and got passed at the net. Sure enough, Austin went on to win her first game, and they were suddenly trading points. Evert had done an apparently "unsmart" thing, and the trend had changed dramatically. Until when? Until Evert tried a drop shot that worked. Having undone her unsmart thing with a smart thing, Evert quickly went ahead, 0–40, on Austin's serve. Until when? Until Austin unexpectedly moved to the net on the return of one of her "moon balls," and smashed an overhead. Smart. Suddenly, Austin's back to 40–40.

Furthermore, as with Ramirez' shot, Austin's strategy wouldn't have had to work to be effective. It only had to announce to the opposition, "Watch out for next time." Had Austin continued to be smart, in this match in which she figured to be and was eventually dominated, she would have purposefully hit the short ball for Evert to come in on, to give herself the occasion to pass her. Were it unsuccessful, Evert still would have had to be thinking, on the next short ball, whether to approach the net and whether Austin would be trying to pass her in the same direction. The player being dominated wants the opponent to be wondering just that.

If the policy fails once, don't revoke it. It may actually succeed in ways you have yet to know about. Approach the net on his second serve and should you get passed, do it again. You may not even be required to make the volley, since, now that he's aware that you're coming, the opponent may net his shot. Or you won't need to rush, since he'll double-fault. Or you may have an easy volley on the center of your racquet.

You do it for next time. It's third down, and a foot to go from the seven-yard line. You try a pass and it fails. But next time, the defense must be thinking about it, and can't put all their men on the line to guard against the run. And that's why the chances for success the next time are increased whatever you do, pass or run, since if the defense has to bear in mind the possibility of a pass, you can more successfully run.

In chess, it's very difficult not to be affected by the speed at which the opponent moves. The faster he is, the less in doubt he is or wants to appear to be. But it's not a particularly clever strategy to be that quick, because you either must take your time on occasions when you're in trouble, and thus give notice of your difficulty, or else move more quickly than you want. Therefore, so as not to reveal unnecessarily those troublesome times, you should take your time even when the move is obvious. You do it for the next time.

No umpire has ever changed his mind on a ball-strike call, no basketball referee on a foul call; yet they are always screamed at by the side against whom the call is made. Is every baseball and basketball coach an uncontrollable lunatic, in ignorance of reality? On the contrary, they're so attuned to reality that they know they stand to benefit on the next close call. And even though the referee may be aware of that sinister purpose, it is difficult not to be intimidated and even it out the next time. So it's not the first time that necessarily counts.

In men's singles at the end of 1977, an unusual situation arose. Three players had a legitimate claim to being No. 1 in the world. Connors, who had been the "man to beat" for the past few years, had been finishing second in a number of tournaments. Borg, who had beaten Connors at Wimbledon, went into the U.S. Open seeded first. Vilas asserted his claim by winning the most tournaments of the year, including the U.S. Open over Connors. The final tournament of 1977 (although it occurred in early 1978), the Grand Prix Masters, didn't help decide matters. (This was the tournament that created quite a stir, because both Vilas and Borg forfeited matches that were inconsequential.) For while Connors beat Borg in the final, and Borg had beaten Vilas in the semifinals, Vilas had beaten Connors in the "round robin." Interesting to note was that this particular circle would have resulted in a different winner had the schedule of the tournament been different. Assuming the winners of matches would have been the same, if Borg had met Connors in the semifinals, Vilas would have emerged the victor, since he would have then beaten Connors in the finals. And had Connors met Vilas in the semis, Borg would have won, since his victory over Vilas would have come in the finals.

Confusing? Quite, but indicative of the whole year's play, and indicative of a "triangular" phenomenon that occurs quite frequently in sports, and which has never been properly analyzed. And I think such phenomena attributable to erroneous conclusions drawn from first-time occurrences.

Connors beats Borg, Borg beats Vilas, Vilas beats Connors. That's the triangle—and the pattern holds, not only in that tournament, but for at least the year. Often we are led to believe that when these triangles exist, they are due to differences of "style." If, for some reason, Kansas City can always beat Oakland, but, measured against any third team, Oakland is clearly superior, it is supposed to result from some special pressure, or similar individual characteristic, that only the Kansas City defense puts on the Oakland secondary. Or, if Jimmy Young can beat George Foreman, who can beat Ken Norton, who can beat Jimmy Young, it is because Foreman is not supposed to be able to go against a "boxer" like Young.

I find such explanations wanting. If, for example, Norton's a brute who can't box, which would explain why Foreman can beat him, how can he beat Young when a bigger brute (Foreman) can't? Or if Norton's a boxer who's better than Young, how is it he can't outbox Foreman when a lesser boxer (Young) can? It's theoretically possible that particular characteristics may exist in sufficiently complex permutations to permit such triangles, but I am skeptical whether they provide the simplest of explanations.

As will be discussed in greater detail in Chapter 10, superiority owes a lot to a belief in that superiority. That belief can be largely formed from a first-time occurrence, one that we've seen has quite special characteristics.

I think I know how the Connors-Vilas-Borg triangle arose. Connors would probably have beaten Vilas by coming to the net. At least, that's how he had easily beaten him the year before, how he was beating Borg, and, judging from the superiority Borg seemed to have over Vilas, how he should have beaten Vilas in the U.S. Open. But in the Open, Vilas passed him. So Connors stopped coming. He had done the same against Orantes a couple of years earlier in the Open, and had lost in straight sets. Now it is true that both Vilas and Orantes are particularly good at passing, Vilas with top-spin backhands cross-court, Orantes with top-spin forehand lobs, but so is Borg, and so are lots of others. However, I don't think they had proven them-selves good enough to take away the advantage from Con-nors' net game. (Borg may have changed things since then, but at this point Connors still had a clear superiority over him, while Borg continued to dominate Vilas.) But Con-nors thought so, against Vilas and Orantes, because he stopped coming to the net. And that's why he lost, not be-cause some "styles" produce funny triangles. It may be true that some styles fare better than others against some other styles, but rarely to the extent of violating the law of transi-tivity: If A is better than B, and B is better than C, then A is better than C. When it fails, it fails for other, more psychological reasons, one of which I have just described. Connors lost because he stopped coming because he thought he would lose by coming, because he didn't give it enough of a second try. He lost not for the reason (getting passed) that he thought he would lose, but for the-reason-that-he-thought-he-would-lose (it is interesting how the language can't easily make that distinction). With another opponent, that sequence didn't occur; he made it the first time, so he didn't get to the point of doubting himself, so he didn't doubt, so he didn't lose.

If your game, like Connors', depends on your coming to the net, or depends on something you recognize, do it. Be prepared to lose, if there's an effective counter-weapon that can be used consistently. But you should give the opposition every opportunity to demonstrate its inconsistency, and to accomplish that purpose, once is not enough. Can you imagine how happy Vilas must have felt when Connors stopped coming?

IN EXTREME CASES, FIND ONE THING
THAT WORKED FOR YOU

In clinical practice, a last resort in attempting to help highly resistant clients is to try to discover what has been effective for them in the past in reducing some of their symptoms. In full recognition of the dangers of this analogy, I would still suggest that when nothing seems to be working for you on the tennis court, try to recall one particular sequence when you won the point, and then see if you can duplicate it. If it turns out to have been the one that trickled off the net cord, good luck.

CHAPTER 7

Individual Differences: Personality Types

The professor was struggling through his early 40's, and his life seethed with changes. After 16 years at Harvard, he was contemplating a move to Yale.[1]

There are two types of people in the world. One says "Leave me alone, I'll do it my way, I have to concentrate," and the other says "Hey, let me try it his way, I can always go back to whatever I was doing if it doesn't work." The first hates manuals on how to do things, the second is curious. The first has to work a lot harder, but makes fewer mistakes. The second initiates activities and doesn't care so much about what other people think. The first thinks little of himself and little of the world, but a lot about his relationship to the world. The second thinks a lot of himself and a lot of the world, but little about his relationship to it. The first is a defensive tennis player and the second is an offensive one. As to who predominates when they meet on the tennis court, it's hard to say. The best offense is a good defense and the best defense is a good offense.

If you come to psychology to discover what type of person you are, you're in good company. "Typologies" have been around for as long as psychologists thought they could identify anything, and represent a way of accounting for what becomes evident as soon as one tries to discover or

[1] L. Bennetts. "Psychologist Studies the Storms That Come with the Changing Seasons of Life." *The New York Times,* March 11, 1978, p. 11.

apply a general principle: that there are individual differences. Not everyone is the same. "Typing" is an effort to make sense of those differences, to avoid having to say, since not everyone's the same, that everyone's different.

The reason I've invented the typecasting system above is that there is great trouble with all of the others, much of which goes unrecognized. If you attend only to some of the more classical ones, you will discover that you're an endomorphic, viscerotonic, oral-biting, sensing, hoarding, sharpening, field-dependent, mover-away-from-people. These descriptors are intended to be an improvement over Hippocrates' ancient system of determining your psychological type by figuring out what kind of fluid predominated in your body. (Dominated by phlegm? Why, you're phlegmatic! Bile? You're bilious!) The latest scale, attempting to classify us into high and low "sensation-seekers," has gone through seventeen revisions and now has some four hundred questions to test whether you like stimulation or you don't.

Which seems to me a bit too many, and that is the cause for my suspicion. While many might find such descriptive categories appealing (Why it's you and me, Horace!), as a way, perhaps, of seeking to understand interpersonal difficulties (So that's why we could never get along; he always wanted things the same, and I always wanted things different), the existence of even as many as two questions on the scale should make us wonder whether a general system of typing people has been found. Either the person who likes to walk in cold air is the same one who likes many sexual partners, or you haven't found a real sensation-seeking scale to categorize us. At least Hippocrates had a single way of typecasting, however faulty it proved.

We apparently vacillate. We're many things. Sometimes the situation controls much of what emerges; sometimes we're many things despite the situation. People are complicated. They change. Styles change. We don't get clear-cut differentiations. The categories are too restrictive.

Either that or the categories are so broad that everyone fits. An example of a typing system of this sort is suggested by the quote at the beginning of this chapter. It refers to a popular field of psychological study these days, adult development. From the work cited by the *Times* article, that of Dr. Daniel Levinson, to whose life the quote actually refers, it appears that adults typically go through a period of crises and transition periods, and we can all identify ourselves by reference to a particular stage. (It was this psychological research that Gail Sheehy's popular work, *Passages*, was based on.) And the appeal of such works rests in the easy manner in which everyone can identify with this model of change and transition, for if moving from Harvard to Yale is a crisis, then everything is something and everybody's doing everything, even if it's nothing.

When do adult crises or transitions occur, according to this model? Typically, around significant age periods, like twenty, thirty, and forty. How much around? Up to about three years. Even without adding such obviously critical age periods as twenty-five, thirty-five, and forty-five, it can safely be said, by such definitions, that 70 percent of us are currently in a transition between one or another of these periods.

In other words, we can see that typing systems may make arbitrary classifications. Furthermore, the need to find types runs counter to the scientific tendency of seeking generalities, one that in the social sciences, at least, may be gaining in popularity. In the area of gender differentiation, for example, a topic of some psychological and political interest recently, we certainly seem to be moving more toward uncovering commonalities than exposing differences. The results of anthropological investigations in different cultures, scientific work on hormones, political movements in general, and psychological studies of development support the idea that aside from a thing (or two) that men (or women) have that women (or men) don't, we all seem to differ much more in degree than in kind. Even the great classificatory science, biology, with all its many species, genera, classes, and phyla, distinguishes only until it finds the connections. Birds, it seems to be turning out, are what evolution made of dinosaurs.

So, with one exception, I think I'll stick to my observational system. There'll be no attempt to uncover what stage of life the drop-shotter is at or how the High Sensation-Seeker behaves in doubles, or what the constant talker's early nursery-school life must have been like. Yet, because our experience so often invites careful scrutiny of various "types," because we do seem in everyday life to meet with people who can be described generally and responded to familiarly by others who have not met them, because literature presents to us particular representations of complex human beings under the presumption that the particular is not unique or we wouldn't be able to recognize and respond to it—for these reasons I will describe, in the latter part of this chapter, some types with whom I'm quite familiar. They will be presented, however, without the weight of traditional or recent psychological categories (except, for those who might be interested or experienced in them, in a parenthesis and a footnote). If in the course of depicting some of my favorite opponents, a hint of some general psychological dynamic seems to be present, or an analysis can be made of who is doing what to whom, then I will be more interested in that interaction or dynamic than in any alleged stylistic difference between the participants.

INTROVERTS AND EXTROVERTS

The one exception mentioned, a distinction from the psychological literature that I do want to focus on for a brief time, is the dimension of extroversion-introversion. The types were originally introduced by Carl Jung, a student of Freud's and later founder of his own school of psychoanalytic thought, and have recently gone through an interesting evolution. There appears to be the possibility that different behaviors may be attributable to different types of nervous system.

Introverts, who are more inner-controlled, or -dominated, or -focused, or -motivated, according to the original distinction, seem to be able to concentrate on an activity for longer periods of time. Extroverts, who find external stimulation more to their liking or more a source of their identity, seem to take more "involuntary rest pauses." Introverts are more vigilant, less susceptible to outside influence. Extroverts are more distractible, more interested in whatever's going on around them.

This distinction invited the hypothesis that introverts, if they were matched for intelligence with extroverts, would do relatively better than extroverts on the second half of tests. The reasoning was that extroverts would tend to get distracted, and introverts would "stay with" the task longer. It is this hypothesis, supported by empirical studies, that I think deserves testing on the tennis court. That it emanates from a typology that is at once old and new, one that gibes with much of our experience and, of late, has been related to biological differences, and one that, while it sounds simple, is sufficiently complex to permit the diversity of our behavior referred to earlier, suggests that it may be an important result of whatever individual differences can be scientifically supported.

This hypothesis should imply that in tennis, when an extrovert and an introvert of relatively the same ability play, the extrovert must build up an early lead to win. The introvert will be more likely to come from behind. If the introvert can stay relatively even at the beginning, it should prove to his advantage.

The first and major problem is that there is no easy way of determining which type one is. The popular descriptions, however, are not very far from Jung's initial conception and the distinctions already referred to. Extroverts, who tend to be involved in a variety of activities, think of themselves as "broad," compared to introverts, whom they regard as "narrow." Introverts, who tend to be perseverant with a single activity, think of themselves as "deep," compared to extroverts, whom they may regard as "shallow." The common picture of the introvert is one who is content to be alone, with few but deep relationships and interests, and of the extrovert is one who moves around more, who wants to be with others. The introvert defines herself in terms of her own aspirations and needs, the extrovert in terms of others' expectations. When the introvert is depressed, she locks herself in her room; when the extrovert is depressed, she gets on the telephone.

If these brief descriptions are not altogether helpful in discerning which type you are, it is quite understandable. As with other types discussed, some would think the categories too narrow—that there is more to their personality than can be contained in either type; others would think them too broad—that anyone could find herself in either one. If one tries to place the two types on the tennis court, however, the distinction certainly makes some degree of sense. One kind of player shows little outward sign of emotion. She is concentrating. She is inscrutable. The other cannot stand all that internal control. She is gesticulating, talking, "playing to" the audience. To those four-hundred-item-questionnaire psychologists who might find this system of identification a little too simple, what can I say except that theirs is too complicated?

By this simple criterion, who would be more extroverted than Jimmy Connors, who engages in dialogues with the crowds, who does dances with his hips when he escapes narrowly, who sometimes even wags a finger at his opponent (who but Ilie Nastase, that is)? And who would be more introverted than Bjorn Borg, he whose only show of outward concern is a slight curling of the lip when he double-faults, whose expression, as every television commentator is forever reminding us, never changes? Armed with my hypothesis, I closely examined the matches that Borg and Connors, currently the two top-ranked men's players in the world, have played against each other.

If the introvert can hang in there at the beginning, he will win, the hypothesis states. If the extrovert does not build up an early lead, he will lose. There are problems of definition, not least of which are the meaning of "early" and how much of a "lead." But in the first match between them that I looked at, the 1978 Grand Slam won by Borg, 7–6, 3–6, 6–1, there were at least three clear ways in which the extrovert did not "come back." In the first-set tie-breaker, Borg won the first point on Connors' serve. He went on to win, 7–1, a quite graphic demonstration of the importance of what happens early. In the first game of the third set, Connors lost his serve, and proceeded to lose the set decisively. And finally, although Connors came back to win the second set, he couldn't come back to win the match after losing the first set. It's as if, when something goes wrong early, the extrovert were saying to himself, "What are they saying about me out there? I'm just terrible," and is eager to leave the scene, and the introvert, more attuned to his own drummer, doesn't have that concern.

I then made note of some of the more famous matches between Connors and apparent introverts. (A further way of identifying introverts on the court, perhaps ironically, is their popularity with the crowd. It's easier for the inscrutable to get a reputation for being "good guys" than it is for the demonstrative players.) When Arthur Ashe upset him at Wimbledon in 1975, it was after Connors had lost the first set. (Ashe is inscrutable on the court.) Against Manuel Orantes, the heavy underdog, in the U.S. Open finals of 1975, Connors lost in three straight. (Although Orantes doesn't look inscrutable, his facial expression never changes. He's always smiling the same smile.) Against Rod Laver in the infamous "Winner-Take-All" (but Loser-Take-Some) match in Las Vegas, it was a Connors victory after taking the first two sets. (Ever see Laver talk to the crowd?) In all instances, if Connors won, he streaked to an early lead; if he lost, he was behind early.

More systematically, I reviewed the scores from all the Connors-Borg matches. At the time of this writing, they have played fifteen times, and Connors holds a 9–6 lifetime lead. The principle requiring testing is whether Connors must build an early lead to win.

There are a number of ways in which you could try to seek confirmation of the hypothesis, but each has problems. For example, you would expect more Connors victories in straight sets (indicating he had built and held an early lead) than in split sets (indicating either that he was not in the lead at some point or that his lead had diminished), were the hypothesis true. But since the probability of a straight-set victory—if two players are of equal ability— is much lower than one of split sets, the comparison is not very meaningful. (Connors has actually won five matches in straight sets, four in split sets.) Additionally, a straight-set victory by Borg is supportive of the principle, since it means that Connors did not come from behind. It is then apparent that a straight-set victory by Connors, a straight-set victory by Borg, and a come-from-behind victory by Borg are all consistent with the hypothesis. The one thing excluded is a come-from-behind victory by Connors.

Although the two have played forty-five sets, there has been only one occasion when Connors won the match after being down by a set to Borg (and that, the second time they ever played).

Here is another way of seeking confirmation, the "turn-around" test. According to the hypothesis, the introvert should win relatively more than the extrovert by turning around a situation when he had fallen behind early (once losing, the extrovert loses). If we identify a "streak" ratio as the number of times a winner of a set wins the next set, compared to the number of times it "turns around," we find that in Borg's wins the streak ratio is 4:9 (and three of those four have occurred the last two times they have played), while in Connors' wins, it's 10:7. Borg's victories, in other words, have been marked much more by "turn-arounds," relative to streaks, than Connors' wins.

In these two major systematic ways (as well as through the information provided earlier), the principle certainly seems to hold and to be worthy of further investigations. Not only might we, as a result, finally confirm a general distinction between two types of personality, but we might be able to make predictions to the tennis court from that distinction. Rarely is anything from the "scientific" branches of psychology so directly applicable.

MY FAVORITE OPPONENTS

From some empirical research on individual differences, we move to simple observation and the attempt to depict the structure of interpersonal dynamics. Not by data-collecting alone do we extract familiar patterns of behavior. If some would argue that the following are quite unfamiliar or at least have no place in a chapter on "types," I would assure them that while I may bring out what is normally hidden in my partners, others have certainly met some of them before. If so, they properly belong here, alongside the bilious and the phlegmatic, the high and low sensation-seekers, the Capricorns and the Gemini (whose absence is not accidental):

THE PROFESSOR (Reverse Oedipal) [2]

He smokes his pipe onto the court and introduces himself as Dr. So-and-So. He would wear his tweeds onto the court also, except that nobody wears tweeds in the classroom anymore (except Ronald Colman on the Late, Late Show, and some ambitious assistant professors in the Ivy League). In fact, the change in men's fashion to turtlenecks in the last decade has really brought him into his own, since turtlenecks can be worn under a warm-up suit until the last minute of practice and sometimes beyond. He thus need never relinquish his identity. And doesn't. Even without his uniform, he can always be identified once he's started to play because of his two outstanding professorial traits: he's excessively tolerant and he carries his grading book with him. He's usually smiling, especially ingratiatingly after he's won the last game before the changeover. "Boy, you almost had me there for a minute, the way you were hitting that line," he will patronize you with. And it's not only "nice shot" (B+) that he grants you, usually when you pass him at the net when he shouldn't be there, but he has a racquet-and-hand clap above the head ("A"), and a waved finger at you when the net ball that he couldn't have got anyway goes by him (a gentleman "C" which, although you don't deserve it, he gives you to prove his gentlemanliness).

There is no failing his course, since you always get praise for your effort. His stature, never being in question, doesn't require, indeed cannot assimilate, anything informative.

---

[2] The Oedipal conflict, in men, is represented as resistance to authority, whatever the basis. Here exemplified is the universal authority, whatever the issue.

Try to tell him a thing or two about the number of back-hands he's hit down the line compared to cross-court and you'll quickly learn the historical background of this habit, which he's long ago consciously adopted, and the exceptions that you haven't noticed.

He'd be a curious enough vestige of some pre-Cambrian Age were it not that he takes himself so seriously. As he is, he makes you want to lunge for every ball and smash it toward his Adam's apple, but you refrain, knowing that he'll block it, probably with a mishit, and forgive you.

THE STAR (Genital Exhibitionist) [3]

Nothing is too good for Madame. Her plum warm-up suit is by Ultra-Sport, her racquet is weighted with graphite at the bottom for extra control, and her hair, even as it is tucked under her Katasha headband, is a model of studied casualness. She early on learned the principle that if you have enough form, you can dispense with a good deal of content. But since she doesn't know she learned that, she's continually at odds with herself for not being as good as her form would indicate. "I don't know what happens to me—I'm all right until I get into a game," she thinks she has discovered. "Must have something to do with not wanting to outdo my mother."

She always plays in the front court most visible to spectators. Her movements are exquisite, especially on the low cross-court forehand, which she hits with her head at a 45° angle from the ground and perfect side-spin. She makes this shot on at least one out of ten tries, the other nine sailing over the court divider, or, when she's on, into the bottom of the net.

She's impossible to play with, not so much because you

[3] One whose pleasures are derived mainly from displaying herself and calling attention to her own gender and sexuality.

spend most of your time retrieving the ball from the surrounding countryside, but because she seems to be doing it deliberately. The harder she tries, the worse she gets, and the worse she gets, the harder she tries. Since she is often a recent victim of popular therapy, she is determined to prove that she has a Perfect Right to Everything. She could no more heed the sensible advice to take a little speed off it, or just try to get it into the court, than she could become a pig-tailed, acned teenager again, attracting little attention. So she carries on, hitting two of three opening rally shots into the net, then trying it the backhand way, and when she finally succeeds in passing you with one of those crisp ones, the expertise she knows has been hiding all morning is confirmed, and permission is thereby granted to start another series of balls sailing in all directions. When games are played, her form is still perfect, especially on those occasions when she misses the ball completely.

MR. NONCHALANCE (Passive-Aggressive) [4]

He wears no turtlenecks or warm-up suits. The best recognition of a change in seasons you'll get from him on the court is a switch from his bathing suit to his dungarees. It does not seem a deliberate effort to "psych" you out. He just "doesn't care." As apt as the Professor is to announce his title (and often his rank) before you've shaken hands, so is Mr. Nonchalance likely to tell you nothing, however real your intent and however graciously you try. "What do you do?" you ask him, on your first meeting. "Not much," he responds. "Do you work?" "Sometimes." "Do you come here often?" "Mmm, once in a while."

[4] Unable, actively, to express or fulfill his needs, he insidiously places others in the position of either meeting those needs or appearing to deny him his right to them.

On the court, his dominant theme is "Whatever you like." "Shall we start?" you ask, after fifteen minutes of warm-ups. "Whatever you like." "You sure you've had enough serves?" he wants to know—"Take as many as you like." (He, of course, doesn't need any.) "Shall we toss for serve?" you ask. "It doesn't matter— Why don't you serve?" he responds. What kind of tie-breaker should we play? Whatever you like. Do you want to play a set or just hit? Whatever you like. Shall we ask those two over there to join us for doubles? If you like.

He offers you water from his tennis can, gives you your choice of sides, and always opens up his own can of balls. You sometimes get the feeling that he's deliberately trying to get you to hit one of his shots over the fence, so that he can magnanimously brush it aside and tell you there's plenty more where that came from.

His ferocity emerges after he's let you know that nothing matters. He'll chase down anything. He never gives up on a point. Only when rallying, if a ball is clearly beyond reach, does he slowly shuffle along as if nothing matters.

It is extremely difficult to perceive him as the tiger he is, since he has early on convinced you that everything's up to you. He is impossible to win against, since you must then be able to take seriously what has already been shrugged off. If you score more points, it doesn't matter. If you score fewer, you haven't even been able to win against someone not really trying.

And that's the power he has and needs. If the opponent is pretending not to care, how do you show you do? As his cryptic replies to your simple questions are an attempt to disguise just how important he thinks he is, so the laissez-faire attitude is a disguised form of control. Who else but someone taking it so seriously would spend all this effort to take it so lightly?

MS. GENEROSITY (Double-Binder) [5]

She has a lot of hustle. During warm-ups, she's chasing down balls as ferociously as Mr. Nonchalance, especially the ones on your side of the net. "I've got it," she shouts, after waiting for you to take a step or two in its direction.

She manages to synchronize her opening shot precisely with yours, so at the beginning of rallying, balls are being served from two directions simultaneously; in the middle there is a good deal of stopping and starting; and toward the end, there is a ten-second pause between balls, until you step in and take the plunge. She performs similarly with players on adjacent courts. You have two seconds to retrieve her ball before she goes flying after it and flying back, saying "excuse me" once in each direction. As you guiltily shout, "I would have gotten it," she smiles and, with a you're-too-important-I-wouldn't-want-to-interrupt-you tone, says, "That's all right." On the next occasion, she does say "thank you," *sotto voce*, and allows you three seconds to retrieve before taking off again.

As a doubles partner, Ms. Generosity can reach all balls, except the hard, low one hit just to her side of the center stripe. This one she makes a slight head feint for, enough to dissuade you from participating, then withdraws from once it has gone by, as she looks to you for it.

As a planner, she never initiates the arrangement, always responds to it, and only barely hints at the things she's being torn away from to join you. "Wednesday, Wednesday, let's see. . . . I do have a dentist appointment in the morning, and I was planning to visit David's teacher in the afternoon. . . . Uhh, sure, eleven A.M. would be fine, I can switch things around."

---

[5] One who sends you two strong, conflicting messages—I need you, and I can do very well without you—at once. Should you respond to one, you get hit with the other.

"Listen, are you sure?" you reply. "It really doesn't matter to me when we play; I'm free the whole day."

"No, no, eleven would be fine . . .'"

"Okay, see you Wednesday, then."

"Uhh, do you think maybe you could play at three . . . ?"

"Yes, I'm sure I can, if that's better for you."

"Well . . ." (now replace dentist with gynecologist, and David with Susan, and take it from the top).

All effort goes into disguising what she wants. Facial expressions, voice tones, and third parties ("Do you think they'll get our ball for us, or should we go ourselves?" she says to her partner, loud enough for her neighbors to hear) are common devices. Anything but a direct expression of her desires. For if Ms. Generosity expressed her intentions directly, they might be refused or negotiated. And her generous nature wouldn't know how to tolerate that.

THE EXPERT (A Leveler)[6]

As someone once said of Socrates, wherever you go, you meet him on his way back. As we parted play last week, he asked about what I had earlier told him I was busy doing, writing a book on tennis and psychology. "How's your book coming?" he wanted to know. "Okay," I said. "I just finished a rough draft." "Hey, terrific," he responded. "By the way, have you seen this book that's just come out, —————*on the Tennis Court*?" "No," I tentatively said. "What's it about?" "Ohh," he murmured, "just some psychological analysis of the game. Written by a couple of shrinks. Heh, heh."

The Expert uses graphite because it's the only racquet that cures tennis elbows, and because Tony Roche has testified to its healing powers. This he tells you just after you've informed him that you've switched to fiberglass be-

[6] One who sees no differences in others' experiences and reduces them to his own.

cause of your elbow problem. He also has a five-minute-a-day exercise for you that's sure to work, a special salve that's better than all the arm bands, and advice like taking aspirins half an hour before you play (for stamina, it's a banana half an hour before).

He knows how to serve properly, how the feet should move on the volley, how to turn when hitting the overhead. He's familiar with the Eastern grip, the Western grip, the Continental grip, and he knows when each should be used. He doesn't hesitate to point out to you why you're having trouble with the elbow—it's because of the wristy, top-spin backhand that you always hit. His own form is, to say the least, highly unorthodox, but that's because, as he's also fond of telling you, he learned it wrong to begin with and is stuck with it.

Only when you realize that he's always partially right, that you do have a wristy, top-spin backhand, but also a sliced, underspinny one, can you begin not to take his word on everything. Like a beginning player, the Expert can see similarities, but cannot articulate differences, except in himself. Your elbow, your serve, your book all remind him of—indeed, duplicate—his own experience. Only he is not expected to profit from his advice, because he already knows what you must learn: since his vision is biased and his experience incomplete, the Expert is often wrong.

THE DESPOT (Paranoid)[7]

Unlike Mr. Nonchalance, who overtly asks for nothing, the Despot lets you know rather quickly that he demands everything. And does so in a way that makes it quite apparent it would take an armed coup to stop him. "Ball!" he shouts

[7] Filled with a sense of his own importance, his efforts are directed solely at discovering how others are trying to do him in.

the instant his reaches the five-mile limit beyond your neighboring court. And when he retrieves yours, three feet from where he's been standing for the last twelve rallies, it is accompanied by the implicit but quite clear message that you better not let that ever happen again.

The Despot always succeeds in rising near to the top of his local club's rankings. Once there, he manages to maintain his position through a variety of means that would make Machiavelli proud. When formidable opposition appears ready to invade his throne room, he leaves for vacation, or feigns illness, or attends high-level tournaments in foreign territories. When obliged to defend his title, he does so primarily against puppet opposition—he solicitously and condescendingly arranges with the eager but least capable potential usurpers to put his power on the line. Having rigged the battle, he then issues constant press releases, advertising the numerous occasions he has made himself available.

Close control of the local scheduling and of the petitions by which others might announce their challenges enables the Despot to keep his position much longer than his superior counterparts. He always knows who's playing whom, and from a distance spies on the match to try to discover hidden weaknesses. He seeks allies by continually coaching others on their best strategy when they are facing an opponent whom he claims to know well. He is thus capable of developing a loyal coterie of followers, especially among those who don't trust their own powers. Only when others trust each other more than they do him can they become aware that the bulk of the Despot's power rests on turning everyone against everyone else.

His elusiveness is best in evidence when he can no longer avoid the direct invitation of a formidable challenger Next Wednesday, between 2:30 and 3:30, he'll be free—oh, you can't make it, well, call me sometime next month, I'm going to be pretty tied up for the next few weeks. Only when someone is as tenacious as he, and the Despot is forced to face the better opponent whom he has so far successfully avoided, do his truest colors emerge. Behind 4–0 in the second set, after having lost the first, he quits because he has a broken racquet string with no adequate replacement accessible. How such a turn of events could so frequently and opportunely occur is anybody's guess, but since the Despot's effort is largely spent on hiding his own deficiencies, he can be expected to be fairly imaginative about devising and concealing ingenious apparatus. When the image he would like to project is no longer possible to maintain, when someone has outlasted him, when he faces imminent defeat, he knocks the ball over the fence, just prior to match point. You are thus forced either to retrieve it from afar, at maximum speed, or else see the hour end before being able to depose him officially. Even through his last instant of power, he finds it necessary to make you succumb to it.

THE CALCULATOR (Obsessive-Compulsive)[8]

Practice shots must be hit a fixed number of times, and must begin and end on schedule. Ten from the forehand side and ten from the backhand. Six serves in the deuce court and then six from the ad. Only when he has properly completed the full fitness program can he begin the set.

At public courts, he knows to quit four and a half minutes before the end of the hour, so as to be the first on line to replace the "no shows" for the next hour. He has his first sip of Gatorade after the fifth game and, like the professionals getting new balls, another sip every seventh game after. When he reads his Sunday newspaper in the waiting

---

[8] Performing everything in an orderly, even ritualized, fashion, he takes most of the meaning or importance out of events.

area, it is always in the same order and takes precisely the same amount of time. Nothing is left to chance.

Since he knows just how far into the season it takes to redevelop his elbow symptoms, or how long into the hour to get his backhand sufficiently warmed up, he is continually disappointed at any deviation from the schedule. A backhand that is missed, after rehearsal time, is inexcusable. It does not fit into the system. After eighteen ground strokes, or four minutes, whichever is less, he's supposed to have it down. He is thus continually berating himself, throughout the match, for any shot that goes awry. The opponent's game is completely irrelevant to him. Hit the finest of winners, and he's kicking himself for not getting to it. He has never played so badly. His astonishment at his imperfection is constant, whatever the cause. He holds himself—or so he would have us believe—to a higher standard.

When you congratulate him afterward for his fine play, you become subject to a litany of failures—he was okay on the forehand, but his volleying was terrible, his serve left him in the third game of the second set, and he'd have been better off in bed.

He has never had an "on" day, and never will. His only recognition of your presence consists of becoming particularly irate when you tell him that the ball near his sideline belongs to the players on Court 2. "I know that," he shouts to you. (He was merely waiting to be within two and a half feet of it, a circumstance that hadn't yet arisen during the previous twenty-four rallies.)

To secure himself the proper opponent—one can't be too casual about these things and trust simply to circumstance —he advertises not only on the club's bulletin board, but in the newspaper. It's a good thing for him that he pays such close attention to the proper method and details of placing notices, for he must do so quite often.

THE PSYCHOANALYST (Voyeur) [9]

People don't dream of tennis racquets any more than they do of phalluses, he informs you as you walk off the court together. They're too important.

The Psychoanalyst has derived a psychoathletic theory of development, which accounts for all behavior on and off the playing field. Freud was okay, he tells you, but mistakenly attributed too much attention to sex. Sex, itself, you see, is merely playing tennis in bed. Certainly it's not by accident —you don't expect—that getting warmed up, whipping the racquet around, and defending against penetration of the zone you've left open bear certain graphic resemblances to other, more Freudian, activities. He stops short of advising you to rush the net if you want to cure impotence and to stay back at the baseline if your problem is premature ejaculation, but not by much. Eventually he writes a book on tennis and psychology, the thesis of which is that you can cure all your maladies off the court by paying proper attention to your symptoms on.

As deep or elaborate as is the Psychoanalyst's analysis of your game, so is his blindness to his own. To uncover his particular area of expertise, you need only discern what he knows least about. If he bores you to death, he's an expert in creativity; if he can't get along with anyone, he specializes in group dynamics; and if he never asks about your children because he's forgotten you have any, his field is child development (and his subfield, probably memory). And if he always manages to secure the best court, best partner, and best deal, and to ask you for a dime for the parking meter or the phone booth, you can be sure he's a social activist of Marxist inclination.

As you get set, following a particularly acute demonstra-

[9] Unable to act on impulse, he derives pleasure from observing others' actions, particularly those that surround moments of passion.

tion of his analytic skills, to scream at him that your grandmother had more psychology in her little pinky than he has in all his inkblots, you stop yourself, realizing that the psychoanalyst's behavior is eminently psychologically understandable. Who else but the one most deficient should be the most preoccupied? Who else but the one most defending against his own self-centeredness should most wish to be known as a champion of social justice? Who else but those least capable of acting simply or directly should be so dedicated to providing others the onerous burden of their erudition?

CHAPTER 8

"Thank You," "When You Get a Chance," and Other Forms of Malice

Those of us who have known the pleasure of hitting a top-spin forehand not only cross-court against a net-rushing opponent but also over the far fence, against the wind, into the outstretched palm of a player on the next row of courts, recognize that there are more influences on our game than how much sleep we had and what our opponent is up to. These considerations may be irrelevant to you if you're surrounded more by ball boys than crowds on adjacent courts, but if so, you can ignore parts of this chapter. It is intended mainly for those of us who know that the essential problem in tennis—especially during its era of expansion—is how to get along with your neighbors and still get your balls back. To crystallize the issue, I have chosen to focus initially, and in some detail, on the major dilemma: When do you say thank you? As any student of psychology knows, an expression so prevalent signifies a sentiment as rare.

Tennis is unusual in that you play your game amidst others playing their game, and in that you often become involved in these doings around you. Unless the interaction is perfect, your game can be affected. Chess may also be played in a room with many chessboards, but you don't typically retrieve others' errant chess pieces that have dropped from their board, or watch their play while involved in your own. Even in the most urban and crowded of situations—say, schoolyard basketball—the game on one court is quite independent of the one at the opposite end of the yard.

But in tennis, dependence is inevitable. Your ball bounds toward a neighboring court frequently, theirs passes you in the middle of play. The situation arises not because everyone's erratic, but often for the opposite reason. The shot that is a winner will often be the one that lands at another's net, since it is the one that's sharply angled or hit with sufficient force to escape the limits of your own court's boundaries. In Chapter 3, mention was made of a side effect of this characteristic: that you could lose an advantage you held during a point by the interruption. Another is that the beginner often feels very guilty when this happens to one of his shots, since he often thinks that hitting a ball onto another court has never before happened in the history of the sport. But at this point I want to address the fundamental problem directly—how do you get your balls back without creating psychological trauma?

"Thank you," or "When you get a chance . . ." accompanied by an outstretched arm, are the common, immediate expressions when the ball goes awry. It is a defensive reaction against the opposite extreme, which not even a complete novice would be guilty of: cutting across other playing fields, in the course of play, to retrieve your ball. You must wait. But what do you do while waiting? Forget about your misguided ball completely, and trust that, when they're ready, your neighbors will accommodate you? Obviously, such ingenuousness would take its toll. Anyone who has spent half his court time comparing, to everyone's dismay, the markings on his remaining two balls with those of the other twenty-seven within a quarter-mile radius, can testify to the folly of such seeming gentility. So the most common way of showing concern about the possibility that you can't get what you want immediately, and don't know how long you'll have to wait, is to express your gratitude right away and leave the rest to your neighbors.

But it often doesn't work. "Thank you" at the moment your ball gets over there announces that you want it back now. Rarely are your neighbors in a position to get it for you now. So thank-yous generally cause some resentment. When they're in the middle of a point, or between points but not close to the errant ball, or even just rallying intensely, they certainly don't need the other ball called to their attention. They will get it when they get there. And if not, because they won't have immediately recognized the direction from which it came, "when you get a chance" will not be an improvement. As reluctant as they are to interrupt play immediately for your bellowing "Thank you!" so are they likely to be resentful of your patronizing them with the granted privilege of waiting until they're ready. If you can wait, why don't you? Although you're signifying just-in-case-you-don't-know-whose-it-is-it's-mine, you're premature. There is a time for that indication, but only much later, when your ball has been overlooked for quite a while.

There is only one absolutely correct procedure. Having followed the ball to its resting place at an adjacent net, keep an eye on your neighbors. How to manage this scrutiny while continuing play with your other balls is a neat trick, but any serious tennis player knows that much of the game consists of keeping track of a couple of things—ball in play, opponent, racquet handle, feet, balls out of play—at once. Adding neighbors isn't adding that much. How to manage this scrutiny while not insulting your partner, who may think you are only prolonging examination of the locale of his bad shot to rub it in, is a more serious problem—but not yours. Indeed, if you make it yours by not

watching your neighbors so your opponent won't feel bad,
you will likely lose the ball and more. As with the changed
line call, discussed in the last chapter, you will have given
him total control, and for the wrong reasons.

Now your neighbors have stopped play and are retrieving
their own balls. Is it the time for a bellowing thank-you?
No, again. For if they are proceeding in a different direction, you would be asking them to make a special trip for
you. Were that the expectation, you could have gotten it
yourself, without provoking both their resentment and your
guilt. But even if they are proceeding in your direction,
your "thank-you" is still premature. The alert neighbor,
about to get your ball, cannot help taking offense at the
presumption of your calling it to his attention. So maintain
your vigil. When he retrieves his own ball, what is the direction of his next step? If it is not toward yours, then, yes,
this is the first proper occasion for a thank-you. It should be
loud enough to be clearly audible a court away, but not
(yet) a disappointed bellow. Disappointment would be premature at this point, since there are some instances in which
one's concentration on his own game is so intense—not an
undesirable attainment—that he literally will notice nothing
else. If, however, he does move toward your ball, then still
do nothing but watch and wait. (Again, you may be in the
middle of play with your balls, and this would be a complicated matter, but nobody said this game was simple.) He
reaches it. He stoops. Are you tempted to yell "thank you"
now? Not yet, it's still premature, he may know very well
what to do next. But there is now only one way of showing
it. If, on picking it up, he does something other than turn in
your direction, if he moves his head around in apparent
uncertainty, or cocks his arm without turning to face you,
or pockets the ball, or begins to carry it back to the baseline with the apparent intention of including it in his own

repertoire, then now is the time for the bellowing "thank-you." It may not be done in time, since by now the ball might be in play on his or even a more distant court, but it is a risk you must take, at least the first time around.

Few things are as delightful on the tennis court as the attainment of an understanding between players on adjacent courts, one that does not require constant vocal support or inquiry, one in which each has managed to respect the others' needs without sacrificing his own. There are some who know, five minutes after beginning play, that their neighbors on the left are using Dunlop heavy-duty, those on the right have Wilson 3's, those two courts down have worn-away Spaldings, and those two courts the other way have Wilson 3's, but in block print (last year's batch) rather than script, and this is clearly the ideal to which to aspire. But beware. If you are not alert to such neighbors' ball-recovery needs, you will end up feeling guilty when they efficiently attend to yours, and never know the reason.

ETIQUETTE AND ASSERTION

If all this detail about a simple, trivial event seems to indicate to you an oversocialized concern for what others are thinking, a search for rules which take care of all behavior, a predominant sense of guilt when the bounds of propriety or usefulness are overstepped, and an incorporation into one's behavior of a number of complex and possibly conflicting demands, then you're in good clinical company. This sort of delineation can be viewed, psychologically, as a defense against impulsivity, against acting in ways that some might find inappropriate. But it can also be seen as the necessary result of "civilization and its discontents," a search for prescriptions that minimize the loss of one's own potential gratification when he enters the company of others. Those who most remain themselves, who stay under-socialized, pay an even higher price. They can't get along with anyone, and tend to get locked up.

And if all this concern seems simply a question of etiquette, a set of mannerisms that the elite invent to distinguish themselves from the riffraff, then it is important to consider some social implications of etiquette. For etiquette is not merely a matter of etiquette. Its origin may have lain in obeisance to the frivolities of the nobility—Webster defines it as the "form required by good breeding or else laid down by authority"—but with 250,000 new tennis players a year, and the surface of the earth remaining constant, it now has a different function. It allows the individual to pursue his own interests in a social setting. If I don't have to lean over your plate to get myself the salt, I'm less likely to stick my elbow in your soup. If you can thus pass-the-salt-please, it will prove to both our advantages.

In a social world, the failure to achieve one's goals often results, ironically, from pursuing them too actively. If I jump over everyone to get at the salt, I incur their wrath and alienate them. But failure to achieve goals also results from not pursuing them actively enough. If you're not sure how, when, to whom, and with what degree of volume to make your request, you are likely to be left with rather bland soup. In current "assertion training" circles, the one who sacrifices everyone else's needs for his own is "aggressive," the one who sacrifices his own for everyone else's is "non-assertive," and somewhere in the middle, in "assertion," lies the optimal answer.

Someone who races onto your court to retrieve his ball is aggressive. While he seems to be preventing you from going to any trouble, he is probably creating quite a bit, through his inability to ask for things. Like the one lunging after the salt, only if there's nothing in his path and his timing is perfect is he likely to cause no interruption. And since space and time aren't totally under his control, the likely result is his going out of control when something doesn't go as planned. The person between him and the salt who moves unexpectedly causes the disaster. He then blames her for not being more careful. The person who serves a ball while he's just raced onto her court gets blamed for not retrieving it for him.

Someone who drops everything to return your ball is non-assertive. While she is considerate of your needs, she forgets, delays, or ignores her own. Since invariably her needs inter-twine with those of her partners, they too soon find them-selves being delayed, forgotten, or ignored. If all salt shakers have been passed to the other end of the room in anticipa-tion of needs that don't yet exist, your side of the table gets shortchanged. Partners spend a good deal of time waiting, when she must run after a neighbor's ball even as she holds two of her own.

If the pronouns convey a sexist tone, it is not uninten-tional. Assertion problems occur in men primarily as ag-gression and in women as nonassertion. He can't ask, so takes; she can't refuse, so sacrifices. If that doesn't gibe with your recent experience, it is because lately there has been an overreaction on the part of some. The assertion movement has in fact been abetted by the feminist one. But before everyone settles down to ideal assertion, the pendulum will probably have to move back a bit. Those anxious not to be walked on are currently doing the aggressing. Those who previously were afraid to ask you to return a ball are now ferociously liberated, guilty of three or four premature thank-yous, each a few decibels above its predecessor. And those who were previously stamping over everyone are sometimes, quite mouse-like, overwaiting their turn and satisfying no one.

If you think that issues in relation to one's tennis neighbors have been exaggerated, consider how often their presence becomes a factor in your game. You become annoyed at or distracted by someone from the next court, who is standing, hands on hips, half an inch over your sideline, waiting for you to come across with his ball. Or you lose concentration on your own game, as you wait ten minutes to get your ball back from the neighboring court. Or arguments break out when you respond to the person waiting with a lesson in manners. Or you can't calm down for the rest of the hour, or even the day, when after being quite attentive to your neighbors' Wilson 1's, they have for the fourth time started playing with yours, even though theirs are but a pale, worn-down, unfuzzy replica. It isn't necessary to travel very far from the tennis game to find influences on the tennis game. Attention, motivation, and emotions are certainly affected by what is happening, literally, around us.

There is another tennis neighborhood, especially in congested areas, in which issues of requests, demands, and refusals come up: the one incorporating you and the players still hitting on the court from the previous hour. It's your turn, but they're still there. Resentment is likely to brew in just such an instance, because they are taking something they haven't asked for (a bit more time), you are taking something you haven't asked for (possession of the court), they are giving up something prematurely (the court, before you're quite ready), or you are giving up something that's more than you want to concede (time). Requesting and responding to requests are once again at the heart of assertion and possible to analyze further through the assertion-training model.

Here is a brief summary of the range of assertive responses to this trivial (!) kind of episode:

Aggressive	Nonassertive
1) Moving onto the court while others are still playing.	1) Waiting 15 minutes for the players to notice you're waiting.
2) Continuing to play for a few minutes without acknowledging that the hour is up and others have moved to a waiting position.	2) Moving off the court as soon as you catch sight of someone moving in your direction, even though it's set point.
3) Giving the others two seconds or two points to finish, then moving onto the court without a word.	3) After allowing them the extra time to finish their game, being unable to do anything for 15 minutes, since they are going through 20 deuces.
4) Playing for 15 minutes, once the request for extra time is granted, without interrupting either to make the request again or give up the court.	4) Playing until it's deuce, when your request from 30–40 was granted, and then hastily exiting, because you're taking too long.

As is evident again, both aggression and nonassertion can result in difficulties. In addition, they're possible from both the active and passive positions, in this case, from the person initially making the request to the one considering it. While the assertive response could be added as a third column, let's consider the whole scenario, assertively acted out.

Tristan and Isolde move on to the sidelines at the completion of Dante and Beatrice's hour. D and B (usually D) ask if they can finish the game, since they're at game point. T and I (usually I) say "sure." The game reaches deuce, and D asks if T and I would mind their trying to finish. "No, go ahead," says T, "so long as it doesn't take forever." After another deuce, D says to B, "Look, why don't we play two more points, and if it's another deuce, we'll quit." That is what occurs and D and B move off. T and I say "Thank you," and D and B say "Thank *you!*" And both are right to be grateful.

Implicit in this discussion of assertion is the importance of acceptance and refusal, with respect to both your own and others' requests. The aggressive personality cannot ask because he cannot tolerate refusal; he cannot, in a word, accept "No." The nonassertive personality responds to any request because she cannot refuse, she cannot say "No."

There are similar dynamics displayed in relation to saying and accepting "Yes." The aggressive personality cannot easily say "Yes." Careful as he is in making his own requests, so is he likely to be critical of most others, if theirs are not done in an equally careful manner. Thus, the precipitous request for the errant ball is likely to provoke his resentment. He will not say "Yes" easily. The nonassertive personality, as she cannot say "No," cannot easily accept "Yes." Should anyone show care, she becomes effusive in her gratitude, convinced that the other is wonderful. Thus, to the neighbor who has returned her ball without being asked, she becomes constantly subservient, dashing after the other's at the slightest provocation.

For this discussion of assertion, the emphasis has been on one's tennis neighbors, but clearly with one's partner or opponent, there is ample room for exploration. In general, assertive means being able to ask for things (i.e., tolerate refusal) and be asked for things (tolerate rejection if you refuse). When you can say no to your partner's request (for something to which he's not entitled—extra time, reconsideration of your line call), or make requests yourself (a few more lobs, playing a set), you're on the way to being assertive.

A final point. There is a great tendency for aggressive people to look for aggression, to find it, and to respond aggressively. Even if it's there, the most productive way of reacting is assertively. For the court occupants who are not taking cognizance of your existence, much less your rights, moving onto the court while they're playing can only provoke more trouble. "Would you mind not stepping onto the court while the ball is in play?" or "Couldn't you wait a goddamn minute until we finish the point?" would be common, and only the verbal responses. Not that you wouldn't in all probability accomplish your purpose of moving them off, but you would do so at great expense, by creating an actively aggressive situation in which agression meets aggression. That, as we may or may not have learned from history, is not likely to yield the solution desired. The only cure for your neighbor's lack of assertion, at either extreme, is your own.

Additionally, the aggressive person often misinterprets the other's action as aggressive. If neighbors don't return your balls promptly, and immediately you consider their behavior to be neglect (ignoring the proper assertive ritual described earlier), then you foreclose too quickly on a possible assertive exchange. For by running onto their court and showing your disgust, you offend the one who was simply waiting until he finished with his own balls, or who was shortly to move toward the neighborhood of yours.

The nonassertive person, on the other hand, interprets no situation as aggressive. If others haven't returned your balls for fifteen minutes, it's because they've been too busy. If they don't respond to your timid "Thank-you," it's because they're properly annoyed that you interrupted them at the wrong time. The only decent way to get one's balls back is to wait for the neighbors to be retrieving their own, and then break the forty-yard-dash record, as you make it to the rear of their court and back to yours, while issuing a few dozen "excuse-me's".

The typical result of being nonassertive is that you end up never playing your game because you're too busy satisfying everyone else. The typical result of aggressive behavior is that you end up worse than when you started. Contrary to the popular theory of displacing aggression (pound pillows instead of bottling it up), many find that if they choose the tennis court to "blow off steam," they manage to accumulate more than they've gotten rid of because of the steamy way they blow off steam.

CHAPTER 9

Risk-Taking

[They] figured the safest way to preserve
capital was to double it.[1]

Sports activity is commonly viewed as an arena for aggressive impulses to be acted upon in a socially acceptable way. From this conception stem both the extreme distaste some have for football and boxing, for example, and their extreme appeal to others. Those who view them with awe see no essential harm in them, and those who don't, find the actual violence of the participants and the vicarious bloodlust of the spectators barbaric.

Often overlooked is that while sports can be found anywhere on the spectrum from violent to nonviolent activities, they also represent, perhaps more consistently, a legitimized form of gambling. Taking risks is an essential part, whether it's sacrificing a knight to gain a potential advantage or trying to serve an ace down the middle. When coaches or players deem it appropriate, they pull their goalie, double-team the big man, try for a birdie, fake the punt, and fake the bunt.

But as sports are more or less overtly aggressive, so do the various options in the team's play book represent differing degrees of gambling. The opportunity to take the

[1] Adam Smith. *The Money Game.* (New York: Random House, 1968), p. 211.

risks just mentioned in chess, tennis, hockey, basketball, golf, football, and baseball imply that there are other, more conservative plays that exist as alternatives.[2] Even the word, "gamble," can be misleading, since it has two distinct meanings: first, to participate in a game of chance or skill in which the outcome is uncertain; and second, to take extreme chances in such an endeavor. My favorite poker-playing idol used to say that the reason he almost always won when he gambled was that he never gambled.

When applied to sports, in general, and to tennis, in particular, such a policy is a bit too simple. As we will see, playing it safe at all times can be quite a gamble. And, as the quote at the beginning of this chapter implies, taking a chance may be the safest way to proceed. I can recall being told, once, by my graduate school advisor to "be careful," when I was about to submit an article for publication that lambasted academic hiring procedures. "Academics don't forget," she said, "and you may be coming to them for a job sometime." After thinking about that for a minute, I replied that I'd been combing my hair and making sure I was sober for my last twenty interviews and the result was that I was still looking for a job. "I think I'll try not being careful for a while," I responded, "and see if that's safer."

Risk-taking is not unknown to sports pundits, but one generally hears only about "playing the percentages." What they are, nobody tells us, nor how to go about playing them. Indeed, the phrase seems only to mean "acting conservatively." When a quarterback doesn't risk an interception, a golfer doesn't risk hitting the ball over a sand trap, and a catcher doesn't risk throwing the ball into center field to catch the runner from first base, they're all "playing the percentages."

[2] In fact, much of the psychological appeal of sports activity may lie in identification not with brute force, but with the various risks or gambles that continually present themselves.

This chapter is largely devoted to investigating such a mythology, to considering the worth of "gambling" (in the second sense) relative to being conservative at various points in a tennis match, to discerning safe plays from risky ones, and to seeing whether psychological dallying with risk-taking in the last thirty years affords us any opportunity of learning something about how we often play tennis and how we might do otherwise. That quarterback, golfer, and catcher may have been playing the percentages or they may have been acting stupidly or timidly.

Among sports, tennis is most susceptible to application of risk-taking principles. The reasons, I think, are twofold. In tennis, you practically always have the option of making a conservative shot or a risky one. The game is unique for allowing that possibility continually. And second, knowledge of what is risky and what is not is for the most part hidden or unappreciated during a match. A basketball, football, and hockey player typically know that if you take a hook shot from fifty feet away or throw a "bomb" to a receiver eighty yards downfield or take a slap shot from sixty feet away, you're likely not to succeed. But how many tennis players are aware during the course of play that what they have been doing the last few games is taking too few chances or too many? Or of what has been influencing them to do that? The common parlance about "low percentage" shots is not nearly enough—most of us, I am sure, being uncertain about what's low and what's high, or when low is no longer low, since it's a function of what has already transpired during the game or point.

When you're pulled off the court, are still in motion, and can't stop in time even to lob, you go all out for a winner down the line. If it works, you convert defeat on the point to victory. And if it doesn't, you haven't lost anything since any other effort would quite probably have been futile. Just managing the ball back when your opponent is on top of the net, and you are pulled off court, will only delay your loss of the point one shot. You might as well gamble with the most difficult of tries—a running, passing shot—since playing it conservatively gives you no chance. If a player flagellates himself on missing this one, it is either because he hasn't recognized the difference between something difficult and something easy or because he has the unrealistic expectation of himself that he ought to be able to do everything, no matter how difficult. Many players, in fact, find that they make this shot, that their best performances occur in moments of desperation because those are the only times they have license to gamble.

The opposite case is more commonly a source of error. We gamble when we don't have to, probably because we don't know we're gambling. We go for winners, not when we're pulled off court, but when we're at the baseline in the middle of the court, when we approach the net, when we serve. A tennis shot is most often missed not because of a loss in concentration, stamina, staying power, memory, or skill, but because it was a risky shot. It may not be apparent that there was good reason to miss, because the shot missed resembles the easier one that "you should have made." The one that was hit wide, for example, was hit hard, low, and at a severe angle. The easier one would have had more margin, both above the net and from the sideline.

Most often, then, the correct question after error is not, "Why did I miss that shot" but "Why did I take that shot?" And the most common answer is because some situations warrant it. For example, take the most familiar situation, your opponent is at the net and you are back at the baseline. You miss your shot by hitting it into the net. When the opponent is at his baseline, you never miss that shot. Is it because he pressured you into getting nervous, or that you rushed or "choked"? I doubt it. You took a riskier shot than you would have had to were he at the baseline. On a normal ground stroke, you can give yourself a good deal of clearance at the net and sidelines. But not so with a passing shot, with the opponent at the net. If it's too high, it can easily be volleyed down, and if it's too much toward the middle, it can be blocked into the opposite side of the court before you have a chance to move back into position. The passing shot must be hit sooner, more quickly, and more toward the sidelines. In this position, therefore, you missed your shot because you took a risky shot, one that was called for in the situation.

To anyone who watches this game, it is apparent that players at all levels continually hit hard, low-angled drives when they should simply hit ground strokes that clear the net with a good deal of margin. If you think the slower speed of a ground stroke puts you at a disadvantage, you are mistaken, because in lofting a ground stroke over the net you have a much greater chance of getting it deep into the opponent's court than you do with a hard, low drive. In other words, we hit passing shots when we should hit ground strokes. This behavior is probably the most common form of unnecessary gambling on the tennis court. (The opposite tendency also exists, but is less frequent. If you find that your opponent is always able to volley your shots away at the net, it is probably because you're hitting ground strokes instead of passing shots—that is, giving yourself too much margin.)

THE RISKY-SHIFT PHENOMENON

Why do we often take riskier shots than we should? The answer is provided by recent psychological research into the nature of risk-taking. Experiments revealed that on a series of hypothetical dilemmas permitting various degrees of risk, groups tended to opt for a more risky solution than did individuals acting alone. The finding held true for different kinds of dilemmas, including one having to do with sports.

While explanations of the phenomenon have not been completely satisfactory, the result has proven quite "robust"—consistent over time and across cultures. People seem to get riskier in groups, a condition known as the "risky shift."

Tennis is often played in the presence of other people, and it appears that risk-taking is more likely to go over big with crowds. (But not so big with front-office management, as we'll shortly see.) Consistency and caution are not generally as crowd-pleasing as dynamic flare. You will less likely be faulted by the spectator for losing through taking risks than through being conservative. That effect that others have on us helps explain why we take chances that we shouldn't, and, derivatively, why so many points end in error.

One might well ask what happens where there is no crowd. Surely, not all of us play to standing-room-only in the grandstand. Shouldn't the risk-taking then be reduced?

Not at all. Except when you're up against a ball machine, there's always an opponent. The tendency is often to try to show him what a risk-taker you are by winning hard, by hitting strong—by taking, in other words, unnecessary risks. This tendency can also be exaggerated by an opponent who demonstrably makes you aware of his own errors. "I'll show you I don't need your help," you implicitly proclaim as you "hit out," in response—precisely the opposite of what you should be doing.

What about players who seem to do better before an audience? How can the risky shift account for that? Quite simply. The finding is that risk-taking is more likely in front of people, not that errors are. If, in fact, you find that you improve before crowds, the implication is that you're generally too conservative and that you ought to take more chances. The propulsion to greater risk that the crowd provides brings you out of your overly cautious game.

A simple lesson follows from the last observation: If you find that you play worse before crowds, you normally take too many chances. Either play with few people around, or reduce the riskiness of your game. If you find you play better before crowds, you ordinarily take too few chances. Either play with more people around, or increase the general riskiness of your game.

UNNECESSARILY RISKY SHOTS

The tendency to take unwarranted risks manifests itself in the temptation to take, aside from the passing shot already mentioned, the following shots:

1. The hard-hit approach shot: This is probably the most common offensive shot missed, but it is rarely focused on as very risky. When it goes over the baseline or into the net, it seems just to be an example of poor form, of a bad error. If, in fact, the question asked were not "Why was it missed?" but "Why was it taken?" greater knowledge of its difficulty would result.

The common "break" in a long point occurs when one player's shot is short. When it comes, it is tempting to move in quickly and try to smash it deep to a corner for a winner. But the approach shot has that name for a reason. It allows you to approach the net, for the *next* shot, since you have already moved well into the court. There is no need to approach the net if your approach shot is being hit for a winner. And hitting it for a winner is quite risky, since there is less distance between you and your opponent's baseline than when you're farther back. For this reason, the approach shot is often overhit. There's less room for it to fall in. The advantage it provides is that it's easier to hit the ball deep. The optimum strategy, therefore, is to hit it with moderate pace, well above the net, deep into the opponent's court. By attempting to hit it for a winner—even though it's dramatic when it works—you lose the advantage and gain the disadvantage.

2. The hard first serve: The most impressive of shots is

the ace. Crowd-pleasing and opponent-intimidating. Yet, unless one is a professional, it's usually a bad risk. If the first serve is hit less hard, there is no second serve for the opponent to look forward to. Additionally, if one has a decent, hard serve, varying its speed is an important offensive weapon.

3. The drop shot: This is the one that gets described most often by television commentators as "low percentage." They are right, though, as will be discussed shortly, nothing is so risky that it should never be done, because the expectation that it never will adds to its chances of success. The drop shot does require great accuracy and the proper pace. If hit too softly or low, it's likely to be netted; too high or fast, and it drops, not out of reach, but in the opponent's lap. In addition, it is probably hit best rather from the middle of the court than the baseline, a spot where a deep approach shot would be a better alternative. Thus, there's little to gain and much to lose with a drop shot—a classic instance, as we'll see later in other contexts, of when to avoid risks.

4. The smashed overhead: While the properly hit overhead is unreturnable and thus potentially the most definitive of shots during the rally, it is also the hardest shot to hit properly. Timing is much more critical than for ground strokes. If you don't perfectly time your hitting of a ground stroke, it will simply not be hit ideally. But since the ball is dropping for the overhead, mistiming that shot can result in a total miss, a shot off the wood, or one considerably wide of the court. We're better off taking a little potential speed off that smash, for the sake of greater accuracy.

5. The passing shot instead of the lob: The passing shot, as mentioned earlier, requires the proper height, speed, and direction. Anything else that's playable may yield an easy volley for the opponent. In most instances when it is taken, however, an alternative, the lob, exists. (I say "in most"

because when a player is running at top speed, the lob is harder to hit.) The height of a lob, as well as its direction, can vary, without making it totally ineffective as with the passing shot. In addition, it sets up that most difficult of shots for most people, the overhead. One should see, therefore, below the professional level, a lot more lobs than one does. They entail a lesser degree of risk than passing shots, and they offer about the same advantage. Even among professionals—where the lob doesn't have as much margin for error since practically all know how to smash it effectively —it is used less than it might be, probably because it is not as dramatic and crowd-pleasing as the passing shot.

PLAYING IT SAFE CAN BE VERY RISKY

In each of the above instances, the less risky shot is the more sensible—the overhead or serve that is not smashed, the approach shot that is hit deep rather than overpowered. Why do we choose the less sensible so often? One answer, the effect of the crowd, has been suggested. But there is another. No single strategy for safety continues to entail the same degree of risk, if practiced religiously. Eventually, it becomes not so safe at all. Here, from the 1977 football playoffs, is an example from two games on the same day.

In both games of the first-round playoffs, the AFC had two well-matched teams. In the first, Baltimore, a rising star with a rising quarterback, was playing Oakland, the defending Super Bowl Champions. In the second, Denver (The "Orange Crush"), with the best record in the regular season, was playing Pittsburgh (The "Steel Curtain"), winner of the two Super Bowls before Oakland. Oakland, which had been a touchdown favorite, was having its hands full with Baltimore. Each time Oakland would score, Baltimore, seemingly at will, would march down the field and score again to retake the lead. It happened a number of times in the second half, and with seven minutes left in the game, Baltimore was ahead, 31–28. Then something that was barely noticeable happened. Had it been more obvious, one might have learned something about what underlies common descriptions such as "They choked," "They couldn't stand to win," "He became tentative." Baltimore changed its risk-taking strategy. And the reason it changed was probably because it suddenly was no longer the underdog, but rather realized it could win. It became suddenly conservative when what had been winning for the team all along was riskiness, successfully taking chances because it was not expected.

Specifically, on the three previous drives downfield, Bert Jones had been passing on first down, and sometimes on second. Since the typical (safe) move is to run on first and second down, and pass on third if you don't make a first down, this strategy was keeping the Oakland defense in a quandary. When Jones switched to the more familiar—run, run, pass—no pass was completed (because now, it being third down instead of first, Oakland knew he was likely to do it) and Baltimore had to punt. This happened twice when Baltimore had the ball late in the fourth quarter, and while its defense had been playing well, it couldn't shut out Oakland completely. Oakland tied the game late with a field goal and went on to win in overtime. But the loss really came because of the change in the Baltimore offense, not because the defense gave up three points. Taking no risk was the riskiest thing it could do, since it was expected. Taking chances had been the safest thing for it to do, since it was unexpected.

Denver was in practically the same position against Pittsburgh in the fourth quarter of its game. It was ahead, 24–21, with possession in midfield. Denver was expected to "use up the clock" as much as it could, especially against a team like Pittsburgh, which had the reputation of grinding down the opposition, of repeatedly outplaying a team as the game went on. It was Pittsburgh's expectation too, and probably would have resulted in the use of a few minutes on the clock and then the attempt, like Baltimore's, at holding off the opposition until the end. But Denver was smarter. On second down, Craig Morton threw a "bomb." It scored a touchdown, putting Denver ahead by 10 points, and it won easily from that point on.

Because running on first and second down often makes a third down unnecessary, running is a safer play. Because of that being true, however, it cannot always be true. Once in a while, you have to keep the opposition "honest." If you always fold your poker hand unless you have outstanding cards, then no one will stay in with you when you don't fold, and your expected gain will change considerably. If you always pass on third down, the defense can have eleven men guarding against the pass. And if you never hit a first serve as hard as you can, or a passing shot rather than a lob, or a drop shot, then the defense has one less thing to worry about and its job gets easier.

THE BASIC STRATEGY:
WHAT'S TO BE GAINED AND
WHAT'S TO BE LOST

To put the point another way, there are risky and conservative options in sports, and success has to do with maximizing opportunities and minimizing expenses. One should gamble in direct relationship to the degree to which the opportunity outweighs the expense. This is an absurdly simple principle, but a commonly neglected one. We are often ignorant of what is a great risk (hitting an approach shot hard) and what is a safe play (clearing the net with ample room, yet hitting it deep). We tend to be excited by the presence of others—even the opponent alone—into trying the riskier play more often than we should. And part of the reason for being tempted into riskiness is that there are indeed certain occasions when the risky play should be tried, ones which will then reduce the effectiveness of certain otherwise appropriate defenses. But we get goaded into doing it more often than we should. (We probably don't have to bluff in poker as often as we think, because the opposition, knowing the possibility exists, tends to keep expecting it on occasion. So long as it's expected, we don't have to do it, since we're only doing it so it will be expected. Nothing is more profitable than sticking to your strategy of only staying in with the best cards when everyone at the table keeps thinking this time you must be bluffing.) If the opponent keeps waiting for that extra-hard serve, you never have to deliver it.

The football example provides another useful way of distinguishing tennis from other sports. I suspect that few spectators recall what Baltimore did during those last seven minutes, but that many more remember that Denver "bomb." Had Denver's risky play failed, I think it would have been quite well remembered, especially if it had been intercepted. A subtle inclination to failing conservatively (as did Baltimore) rather than riskily underlies *coaches'* strategy. They prefer not being vulnerable to the accusation that they gambled and lost. That doesn't sit well with the front office. When faced with the powerful, one is much less vulnerable to the accusation that he played safe and lost, because playing it safe is more commonplace and less noticeable. Thus, ironically, in actively coached sports, keeping one's reputation and one's job is not always a function of adopting the winning strategy.[3]

In tennis, there seems to be much less of that "Monday-morning quarterbacking." For one thing, any individual

---

[3] And certainly, conservatism applies to coverage of sports, in print and on the air, probably for much the same reason. It would on occasion be nice to hear a commentator report that so-and-so is a crummy competitor and gives only a portion of his all. Or someone like Fred Perry, on being asked how he'd feel if Borg broke his Wimbledon record, reply, "I'd hate it. I hope he loses. It's *my* record!"

shot does not loom as large as the intercepted pass. For another, as already mentioned, it's rarely clear what the risky and conservative plays are. And for a third, it's one against one (sometimes, two against two), without coaches in the usual sense. As mentioned earlier, those guys in the grandstand who keep a funny watch on Vilas and Borg during some of their matches, or the World Team Tennis types, who have more of an administrative role, don't get fired for taking chances.

Therefore, the restraints toward conservatism, the restrictions of opportunity that make other sports not as interesting as they could be, are absent. This permits tennis to live up to its dramatic potential by inviting those risky plays which keep the opposition "honest." As we have seen, it may also invite too many of them, a result that explains why most points end in error, in shots being taken that shouldn't be taken.

Thus far, the discussion has centered around the difference in riskiness of certain shots. A somewhat related issue has to do with positioning on the court. Before you take the shot, you already may have decided the extent of your gamble by where you are, since certain positions entail more risk than others. Coming to the net is one; being elsewhere but at the center, between the two sidelines, is another. While these positions are often taken to gain an advantage, even defensively there are times when they are warranted. If you have run up for a short shot, and cannot get back to the baseline in time, you should come to the net, even if you don't want to. If you have sent up a short lob which is about to be smashed to one side or the other, you might as well move off center and give yourself a chance at it (the meaning of having "guessed right"). These are instances where the riskier play is actually the safer play, since the normally conservative play will give you little chance. It's like going for the winner when you're pulled off court.

But in other instances, players who do not have professional ability put themselves at a disadvantage by positioning themselves as if they do. You should not take the net, for instance, if you don't know how to volley. This may sound easy enough, but it is surprising how many players are up there because they think it's expected of them. (I'm not referring here to people who are trying to practice their net-play, but of those trying to perform in the best manner they can to win. Earlier, in Chapter 5, we found that winning and improving are not always the same.) Except for the occasion mentioned above, when you're going after a very short ball and don't have time to retreat, you should come back to the baseline when others, who do know how to volley, would be coming in. I suspect that most volleys are missed because the person coming in is not as quick as he might be, and is thus taking an unnecessarily risky shot.

In doubles, it is wise not to play the classic positions, unless you're classic. Not only does the fourth player (the partner of the one receiving) not need to stand halfway up the court (to take advantage, if possible, of the volley from the third, the partner of the server) but the third player doesn't have to stand at the net. More mistakes are made by competent doubles teams as a result of their being in the classical position from which they are forced to take riskier shots than they can competently make, than by missing shots that they should have made.

As there are times during a point for more or less risky play, so are there times during a game and set and match. The principle that always operates is simple and rational: Take chances in direct proportion to what stands to be gained as compared to what can be lost. However, identifying appropriate occasions for risky or conservative play is not as easy as it might sound, because what stands to be gained often is related to what's expected, and what's expected depends, sometimes, on what chances the opponent sees you take. This bit of circular causation is also what makes the decision about risk more interesting.

The scoring system of tennis is quite peculiar. One, two, three—and you're out. No other sport has so many small units organized into larger and larger units, with the winner being determined by the structure of his victories (sets, games, points) rather than an aggregate of the smaller units. In most other sports, one simply makes a grand tally of runs, goals, or baskets, and counts the winner at the end.

The consequences of such a scoring system produce psychologically fertile territory. You can win fewer points, yet win the match. *When* you win points is most critical. The difference in being demolished (in a game or set) and losing narrowly can be a small number of points. The perception, therefore, of how you're doing can change radically with very little change in reality. Even if one is being devastated, he's never completely without hope, since a turn of the tide always permits him to catch up. (Coming back from 0–40, or from "two sets down," is not nearly as unheard of as scoring five touchdowns in the last two minutes of a football game.) But most importantly, relatively minor changes in the score can and do affect the dramatic tempo.

By virtue of the unique scoring system, I advocate different risk-taking strategies as a function of the point score. The principles are these: When you're losing, you have a lot to gain by changing an apparently large lead into an apparently small one. When you're winning, you have a lot to gain by extending what appears to be a small lead into a big lead. Conversely, you have a lot to lose, as a leader, by seeing a seemingly big lead diminish into a small one. When behind, you have a lot to lose by seeing a small deficit change into a large one. Since one point often separates a perceived big lead from a perceived small one, some points are extremely critical. Since riskiness is recommended when you have more to gain than to lose, and conservatism is recommended when you have more to lose than to gain, risk-taking strategies can be tied very directly to particular point scores.

The points in a game most critical for strategic risk-taking consideration are 30–0 and 40–15. These are the only two occasions when players are separated by two points. Being separated by two points is the only occasion for seeing a single point determine whether a big lead (40–15 is a 3–1 lead, a 75-percent rate; 30–0 is 100-percent success) becomes a small one (one that is only one point). When the lead is 40–0, it does not appreciably diminish on going to 40–15. It is still big. Does it seem silly that a change of one point can have this effect? Does it imply that either the lead wasn't so big to begin with or isn't so small now? Yes; but how things seem, rather than how they are, is the stuff of which psychological principles are made.

Therefore: Play riskily at 0–30 and at 15–40. Rush the opponent's serve, or the net, if you get a chance. Look for the opportunity on every shot. There is a lot to be gained.

Play conservatively at 30–0 and at 40–15. You have a lot to lose (including what the opponent has to gain) relative to what you have to gain. Your big lead will potentially become a minor one.

At 0–40, contrary to some expectations, do not gamble. Many flail away at the opponent's serve, thinking, "What do I have to lose?" The point is that there isn't much to gain. Your opponent knows you're being desperate, so even if you succeed, you've been lucky, after apparently having acted impulsively. And by reducing the lead to (a still big) 15–40, you haven't accomplished much. So you have little to gain rather than "nothing to lose." Additionally, what you do have to lose, should you throw caution to the wind and flail away, is the opportunity of getting to 15–40, which, as is evident from the above discussion, is not casually to be dismissed.

The following chart summarizes the strategy presented so far:

Score	When ahead, play	When behind, play
30–0	Conservatively	Riskily
40–15	Conservatively	Riskily
40–0	Riskily	Conservatively

While one player's best strategy is not necessarily the opposite of the other's, it usually is. Thus, for example, ahead 40–0, one can take chances, since the amount to be lost if unsuccessful—you still maintain a big lead at 40–15 —is small.

Testing the principles is difficult for a couple of reasons. As will be emphasized in Chapter 11, on Statistics, few good records are kept in tennis, and there is no way of knowing what's gone on, point by point, in a tennis match, from any published data. You need to be watching each point. In fact, it helps to watch each shot. In fact, you really need to be doing more than that—you need to decide, for each shot in which you're interested, whether the player was being risky or conservative. I have done it with televised matches a few times and find about 75-percent support for the hypotheses of how to play these particular points. Matches included the Connors-Gerulaitis semifinals of the 1977 Grand Slam, and the Orantes-Gottfried semifinals of the Volvo tournament in the same year.

A better way, perhaps, to begin evaluating these principles is by keeping track of your own matches and of the success of alternative strategies. You may then become more attuned to the difficulties of measuring risk and conservatism, to the necessity of paying close attention to the goal of each shot, and to the importance of the dimension. The difference in degrees of risk sometimes appears so slight that your own play may be the best, if not the only, object of scrutiny. You know what you are doing, if you're watching, better than you know what he's doing, even if you're watching. Is coming to the net always risk-taking? Does hitting a winner always mean a risk was taken? Does an unforced error mean the player was being conservative? Nothing proves that simple, for answers depend on the kind of shot you took, and what you were intending to do with it. If, for example, you simply block a volley into the open court, you have acted most conservatively, although you easily hit a winner. And an unforced error can result from either trying to hit a winner or not trying to do anything but get it back—from being, in other words, either risky or conservative.

The difficulties of measuring or demonstrating conclusively the applicability of the principle, however, ought not to deter us from using it or extending it. When an opportunity is available for more gain than loss, gamble. Don't, when it's the other way around. These are some implications:

1. Strategies at point scores other than the ones mentioned (e.g., 15–0, deuce, 30–15) can sometimes be deduced from the basic principle but are less potentially significant than the "two-point-lead" scores. The reason is that early scores tend to be obliterated, in perception or memory, with further point changes in the game. One does not typically think, "I better win this one at 15–0, because otherwise it's 15–all, from which if he wins one to make it 15–30, I'll have to win the next one or else have to win two in a row to tie." Things are perceptually clearer when 40–15 becomes 40–30: "Hey, I thought I had this game. Now he's one point from tying." And the later scores, like deuce or advantage, tend to seem of equal importance to each player.

Some possibilities, with regard to other point-score strategies, do exist, however:

    a. One who has repeatedly lost the "advantage" in a

game runs the risk of having lost a lot should he lose the game. If this has happened to you, play conservatively. If it has happened to your opponent, play riskily;

b. If you're behind in the set, play riskily at 0–0. When you are losing, there's more to be gained by taking slight command. Play conservatively at 0–0, if you're ahead in the set. There's more to be lost by giving up command;

c. From the general theory of gains and losses and the examples already given, a comprehensive point-score strategy can be deduced. When losing, play riskily on the even points and conservatively on the odd ("odd" and "even" referring to the sum of points played during the game). When winning, play conservatively on the even points and riskily on the odd.

At 30–15, for example, you have a lot to gain by extending your small lead to a big one, and the opponent has a lot to lose. You should, therefore, be gambling, and he should be playing conservatively. The reason for not subordinating the earlier point strategy under this one is that with the less significant point changes, perceptions of the extended lead or lost lead are affected more by the game and set score. It is not as critical to extend a one-point lead to a two-point lead if you're behind 1–5 in the set.

2. A three-game lead in a set is perceptually much larger than a two-game lead. A two-game lead is always one service break ahead. A three-game lead is either a double-break, or capable of being extended to that, unless the losing player holds serve. (Notice that exactly half of what is needed to win—six games in a set—constitutes the margin considered "big." The same is true for the point-score in a game. A two-point lead, with four needed to win, is a significant lead.) Therefore, when down by three games (0–3, 1–4, for example), play a risky game. You have a lot to gain by reducing significantly the big lead to a small

lead. Conversely, when ahead by those scores, play a conservative game. You have much to lose relative to what's to be gained.

3. Be alert to how the "favored" player's gains or losses may differ from the underdog's. For example, the favorite always has "more to lose." The underdog, therefore, with "more to gain," should generally be gambling more often. If the favorite is losing, he should play conservatively. He has little to gain (he's expected to win) and much to lose, so why gamble?

4. Recognize that "changing one's game" can very easily apply to the risk-taking dimension, but it needn't mean moving from one extreme to the other. Even if one can't keep track of a point-by-point strategy, it is useful simply to alternate conservatism and riskiness on successive points. This could constitute a sufficient change from a completely conservative game, for example.

Finally, it may be noted that options change as a result of others' strategy. If you are consistently doing the strategically optimal thing, like rushing the net at the proper time, then it will pay for the opponent to change his strategy accordingly, to follow his serve to the net. If that happens, your optimal strategy changes. Such occurrences are constant in strategic games. They are the basis of statistical decision theory, which seeks a maximizing strategy in light of the competitor's options and his decision-making rules. In fact, what makes competition so interesting to many is this continual reassessment of where one is, relative to the other. (It is also what drives others mad. "How many times do I need to reassess myself?" they ask. Or the sports novice asks of the aficionado, glued to the Sunday football games for 10 percent of his life, how many times he can keep watching the "same old thing." Being able to explain that it's not the same thing at all—that because Jones passed for the goal line, the run's beginning to work, or because Portland has started to switch off, Philadelphia's going more to their guards, or because Goolagong is coming in more, Evert is coming in more—is no small task. Those unaware of the dynamics are not so easily enlightened.)

Were everyone aware of the principles advocated in this chapter, the principles would need to change. You can't forever reply on your opponent's choosing options in such a manner as to fit in with your strategic policies. But aside from changing once in a while just to "keep it honest," there is no need to develop conditional strategies at this point. Universal awareness, even of the Truth, may take time.

WHY SOME PEOPLE ALWAYS PLAY BETTER WHEN THEY'RE OUT OF THE MATCH AND NEVER SEEM TO WIN WHEN THEY GET CLOSE

This brief discussion could have occurred earlier in the remarks made on masochism, but it is more relevant placed here. Even though we often "do ourselves in" in the manner described in the heading, the explanation often lies in the area of risk-taking. People fail and succeed, at times when they previously hadn't, because of a change in their risk-taking approach. They do not *want* to do themselves in. They are trying to be rational, but it's not always easy.

The underdog in a match often loses because he suddenly becomes conservative when he realizes he can win. Precisely this turn of events occurred to Bert Jones and Baltimore, in the situation described earlier in this chapter. And it is another way of accounting for the mysterious "tentativeness" which seems to afflict players at various points in a match, particularly when they have victory in their sights. The question to be asked is, Why the sudden change in strategies?

Some psychological research in the area of "achievement motivation" may provide the answer. It is, first of all, important to distinguish the motive to achieve success from the motive to avoid failure. On experimental tasks, those whose motive is to avoid failure typically choose goals that are either very close—where success is relatively assured—or very distant—where failure would not really be viewed as failure. Those who are motivated to achieve success, on the other hand, choose goals that are a moderate distance away.

The point at which the underdog's strategy changes to extreme conservatism is the point at which his primary interest suddenly becomes avoiding failure. Having achieved enough so that he suddenly becomes aware he can win, he begins to think what a shame it would be to come so close and fail. That thought—according to the results of the research—implies that he will no longer choose moderate degrees of risk, but will choose no risk. He doesn't want to make any errors. He wants to take no chances. He just wants to get the ball back (or "eat up the clock"). He changes the strategy that worked to get him that far. Afraid of failing, he becomes tentative and fails. Earlier, he couldn't fail (being the underdog), so didn't avoid failure, so achieved some success.

Once he is losing by enough so as to have little effective chance in the match, a player will often hit much better. The "pressure" is off. But what pressure? The pressure to avoid failure. No longer being close enough to "blow it," there is no longer a failure to avoid. So he can cease being "tentative," gamble a bit, and achieve a modicum of success.

CHAPTER 10

Self-Fulfilling Prophecies

Running back to her door to retrieve something she'd forgotten, Lois turned the key so forcibly that it broke in the lock. Unable to get in or to get the key out, she got ready, with a sigh, to call the locksmith and the friends with whom she had an appointment. Her sister, alongside her, tried being "comforting":

—"Oh, Lois, you must be so upset."

—"No, no, it's okay, things like this happen, especially when you're in a hurry."

—"Oh, come on, you don't have to hide it," her sister exhorted her. "I know these kinds of things really upset you."

—"No, really. It's not very pleasant, but I'll handle it. I'll just come late. They'll understand."

—"Lois, I'm your sister. You can tell me your feelings. Don't feel you have to put up a brave front for me. Just be honest about how upset you are, and you'll feel better."

—*"I am not upset!"* Lois finally bellowed.

Toward the end of Chapter 6, I mentioned how a belief in one's superiority on the tennis court is an important part of that superiority. In general, such a concept has been studied in a number of connections, some having to do with the genesis of emotional states (such as the one described above), performance on cognitive tasks, the experimental use of human subjects, and the environmental etiology of mental illness. It is the area known as "self-fulfilling prophecies."

IT IS IF YOU THINK IT IS (SOMETIMES)

When students in classrooms are expected to achieve more than their counterparts, they do. They do, despite having been judged beforehand to be equivalent in potential to the other group. When subjects in experiments know or can guess the experimental hypothesis, they tend to fulfill it. They do this despite adequate controls ensuring that instructions be read to them in such a manner as to give nothing away about expectations. The basis of schizophrenia, it has been hypothesized by some investigators, rests on similar application of the self-fulfilling prophecy. Treat someone as crazy often enough and she may become so:

—"Ohh, you know Jane, she prefers to play by herself."

—"Oh, no, I don't, Mommy."

—"There, there, why don't you wait until you're up to it, then you can go play with the other children."

—"I'm up to it."

—"Do you really feel like having some company, Jane dear?"

—"I always feel like it, Mommy. You told me I had to be by myself."

—"Now, you know that's not true, Jane dear . . ."

—"But it is true—*you just said it*!"

—"Now I think you better go to your room, Jane dear, acting like that. You're just not fit to be with other people."

Some people who are better—in technique, form, or experience—prove themselves to be so on the tennis court. But not always. Some people with less form, technique, and experience invariably prove themselves winners. So much for technique, form, and experience.

In a study of group behavior among adolescent males,

Sherif, a social psychologist, discovered a curious phenomenon. It was very difficult, even in a competitive sport like bowling, for a less popular member of the group to emerge victorious over the leader. This result occurred, even without any direct cheating or manipulation of the scoring. The process was simple.

When the less heralded performer seemed to exceed expectations, the result was treated as an accident. When unpopular Joe was ahead of the leader, Henry, everyone thought the event hilarious. "Hey, Joe, you must really be feeling your 'Wheaties' today. Hey, whatsamatta, Henry, were you dreaming of your girl friend?" Until such time as the expected is produced, the exceptions tend to be discarded. The process is similar to that found in the examples of performance in the classroom. The children who were expected to do better were rewarded when they did do better, and the ones whose performance was unexpectedly high were either ignored or treated in a joking manner. Well, Johnny, whatever got into you today?

The explanation of this phenomenon is still, among psychologists, a subject of some dispute. It may be motivation, which tends to increase with praise and diminish with scorn. Perhaps attention to details confirming the self-image is increased. One's memory for confirming data might be greater than that for disputing data—a possible explanation of "extrasensory" phenomena. (Does one recall all the times he thought of someone who *didn't* at that moment telephone?) Or perhaps there is a direct connection, a state of conditioning through which this reward would increase similar productions in the future (like Skinnerian pigeons pecking more frequently when their intial pecks are responded to with pellets of pigeon food). Yet, even if the psychological process is unclear, the result is important. Believing you're good is part of being good.

Such belief in one's performance is related to faith in others' abilities to assist us. In the latter part of the eighteenth century, Mesmer was quite successful with one of the first "laying on of hands." His reputation grew across Europe, and people of means would seek out the great man in an effort to be healed of their critical diseases through his special powers. Mesmer's theory was that there was a special form of electrical energy (literally, animal magnetism), which passed through his body (apparently, his alone) and which could be transmitted to the ill. Later on, as a result of more sophisticated ways of perceiving both electricity and personal magnetism (hypnosis), it became clear that people had indeed become "mesmerized," but only because they thought that's what they were becoming. There is no doubt that from the influence of strong personalities, dramatic changes can result, and Mesmer (appearing in dramatic, magician-like attire, doing his number to dim lights, soft music, and subjects with "hands joined or connected by cords"[1]) seems to have been as fanatic in his determination to lay on hands as his subjects were to have them laid on. Most people have never been hypnotized, but it's not only cosmic "vibration" lovers who believe that more can get transmitted between two people than sound waves or a tennis ball. There is that certain something.

At the present moment in the professional tennis world, I think Vilas is Borgized, Connors is Vilasized, Rosewall is Connorsized, King is Evertized, and Gerulaitis is Vilaborconnized. No doubt things will change, and probably before people get too old or wounded. One of the things that will be interesting to see is when they do. For it will probably correspond with the lifting of one of these spells.

[1] Edwin G. Boring. *A History of Experimental Psychology.* (New York, London: The Century Company, 1929), p. 116.

In a very close Borg-Nastase match a couple of years ago, I can recall the prediction of the television commentator (one of the few who provides some insight into the game, John Newcombe) that if Borg turned out to be the winner, Nastase would never beat him again. Borg won, in a very close match, one in which Nastase had a couple of match points, and the prediction has proven true. Nastase hasn't been close to him since.

Newcombe didn't reveal his reasoning, but we're free to speculate. Nastase had always dominated their matches, Borg was rapidly moving to the top of men's tennis, and all he seemingly needed to do was prove he could beat Nastase once. Take the reins away from a previous leader and it will be difficult for him to get them back again. You're better once you've proven you're better, but until then, you can't really believe it. Once Gerulaitis beats Borg, he may beat him a lot more, and not be as dominated in their matches.

With players of relatively equal ability, it is quite common that one of them predominantly wins. Is it that she has his number, or rather that whenever she gets close, both she and he believe she'll win?

The point at which the tide turns often coincides with the point at which one realizes that she can beat her opponent. This can happen in a series of matches between two players, or within a set, or within a game. Even in instances where each wins her share, the tide of strength may not be randomly distributed, but may occur in shifting directions. Examination of the dynamics of the match often reveals that it hasn't been touch-and-go all the way, but that there has been a series of shifts and counter-shifts, a succession of shot- and point-productions that indicate that one player has been controlling for a time, and then the other. How can this be, except that in the heat of competition, one is continually saying to herself, "Aha!" or "Uh-oh!" that she is continually evaluating her own performance, relative to the other's, and that the very evaluation, positive or negative, gets exaggerated through those psychological mechanisms that result in living up to expectations?

The innumerable occasions, in sports, when one hears of "confidence," or being "tentative," or "momentum" can easily be understood in light of this discussion. The picture one has of oneself is vitally important in considering what picture one comes to resemble. What is confidence except treating the mistakes as aberrations and the right answers as expected? What is being "tentative" except believing that the other is better or more powerful, and even if you made a few right moves along the way, everyone out there can see they really were flukes? What is momentum, except the results of these various beliefs, exaggerated because of the double effects on both you and the opponent? How else to explain not only the skewed results that the Borg-Nastase match illustrates—Nastase winning all matches before and none after—but the frequent occurrence of these kinds of shifts at all levels of play. You beat him regularly until he wins, and then he beats you regularly. You beat him regularly, 6–0, until he wins a game, and then it's always 6–4 or 6–3. He can't get a point at all for the first few games of a set, and then most games are close, once he does. Despite the number of games or points that are played even, despite the match always going down to the wire, he always manages to win. And finally, there's what I've termed the "streak" function, the tendency for points to "cluster" together for one or the other player.

STREAKS

If you kept track of each point in the first two sets of the U.S. Open final in 1977, you would have discovered an interesting phenomenon. (See chart below.) Vilas' points tend to follow Vilas' points and Connors' points tend to follow Connors' points. What you might expect at such a level, or would expect considering that the total number of points won by each player during that time was practically the same (53–52, Vilas), is that the typical pattern would be "C-V-C-V . . ." an alternating of point-winners. Or, if you were somewhat more statistically interested, you might realize that with two players of equal ability, the chances that the same player would win the point as won the last one would always be *50 percent*, that there should be as many clusters (C-C or V-V) as turns (C-V or V-C). (This expectation would have to be modified by the knowledge of who was serving, but observation of the data does not yield the conclusion that the serve was responsible for the cluster. Indeed, in every game except two—the sixth game of the first set and the fourth game of the second— all the loser's points in any one game followed one another directly. And those two games were both ones that went beyond a first deuce, in which case it is impossible not to have greater alternation of point-winners.)

Vilas-Connors Point Score, 1977 U.S. Open Finals
(Won by Vilas, 2–6, 6–3, 7–6, 6–0)

Set 1   (Vilas serving first, Connors wins, 6–2)

Game	Point total V	C	"Streak" ratio
1: V-V-V-V	4	0	3:0
2: C-C-C-V-V-C	2	4	3:2
3: V-V-V-C-C-C-V-V	5	3	5:2
4: V-C-C-C-C	1	4	3:1
5: C-C-C-V-V-C	2	4	3:2
6: V-V-V-C-C-C-V-C-C-V-C-C	5	7	6:5
7: C-V-V-C-C-C	2	4	3:2
8: C-V-C-C-C	1	4	2:2
Tot:	22	30	28:16

Set 2 (Vilas serving first, Vilas wins, 6–3)

Game

1: C-C-V-V-V-V	4	2	4:1
2: V-V-C-C-C-C	2	4	4:1
3: C-C-C-V-V-V-V-V	5	3	6:1
4: C-V-C-C-V-V-C-V-C-C	4	6	3:6
5: V-V-V-V	4	0	3:0
6: C-C-C-C	0	4	3:0
7: V-V-V-C-V	4	1	2:2
8: V-V-C-V-V	4	1	2:2
9: V-V-C-V-V	4	1	2:2
Tot:	31	22	29:15
Grand Total:	53	52	57:31
	(50%)		(65%)

The result of the count was 57–31, or 65 percent, in favor of clustering. (Results of the entire match showed a clustering of about 60 percent.) Although each player won half the points, it was almost twice as likely for the winner of the previous point to win the next point. I had been particularly interested in the match because both Connors and Vilas were making claims on being No. 1 in the world in men's tennis and they had rarely played against each other before. Confidence was likely to shift from one to the other—if self-fulfilling prophecies were true, even at this level—and was likely to be more evident in the early part of the match. The "streak" function seemed to confirm the hypothesis.

My own experience tends to show that over time the score seems to widen between two players of slightly different ability. My closest matches with players who have proven better than I have been the first ones, when, it would seem, nobody had yet known who was better and the shifting tide had little history to stem its turns. At least I think this a more fruitful method of analysis than would be implied by saying something like, "People feel each

184 ⑪ PSYCHODYNAMIC TENNIS

other out at the beginning." If a player is groping, it is for
a belief in his own superiority. What we were witnessing in
the early sets of the Connors-Vilas match, I am sure, was
a manifestation of each player's continually thinking, "Hey,
I'm better; hey, he's better."

If there are still some who doubt that this kind of "streak-
ing" or momentum exists, I would be the first to recognize
that there has not as yet been an adequate empirical demonstration of it, since such proof ought readily to be available by gathering the data or compiling statistical records.
But before gathering, and then analyzing, one needs to
know what to gather, and how to treat his collection. At
this point, I am not altogether sure that all or even most
points will follow this cluster pattern, since there are a host
of other factors operating on one's tennis playing and on
one's psyche, a number of which I hope to have alluded to
in these chapters. The search for an adequate measure of
the "turning tide" is also a justification for inviting players
to be alert to some of the instances in which one can demonstrate that a shift has occurred. Such is the purpose of
highlighting phenomena such as the extension of the margin of victory, or the opponent's always coming close to
you but never quite winning. One more example of this
kind of support for the self-fulfilling prophecy might serve
to illustrate the psychological process that produces it.

On occasion, for one misguided reason or another, I
have wished to be nice to an opponent I could clearly beat
and have deliberately lost a few points. Maybe it was my
department chairperson, who I was afraid would want to
channel his defeated energies into an area of his own power
were he beaten too badly; or perhaps it was a fellow therapist who I was afraid would later get even with me by
pointing out all the ways in which his treatment methods
and results with clients were superior to mine. But I'm sure
that it's an occasion that some of us who are neither overly

masochistic nor riddled with guilt, but perhaps a little bit generous and a little opportunistic, can recognize. We might even be able to compare notes on how to do it convincingly. How do you manage to make sure you miss without missing by a mile? Are pronounced histrionics necessary or do they cause suspicion? The Everyperson Guide to Success Through Losing—must reading for the corporate-ladder-climbing set.

What I have found when this "dumping" of points is done right is that it has a telling effect on both the opponent and the one doing it. I have had to struggle, thereafter, to win. One occasion I can recall being so nice was the first time playing against someone I had known socially. Soon it became clear to me that I was the better player and, after getting to 4–0, I decided to try to lose a game so my opponent wouldn't feel so bad about being "shut out." I ended up winning, 6–4, with a lucky net cord off the top of the tape gaining me the victory on set point. My deceptions, practiced so as not to make what I was doing so obvious, were apparently so well-executed that not only did he gain in confidence, but I began doubting myself. This turn of events occurred even though I was aware that I had initiated it on purpose. His growing stature diminished mine, even though I had deceived him into thinking his game "really" was improving. It wasn't initially, but it was later, based on his having thought it so initially. The self-fulfilling prophecy is particularly evident on the tennis court because it's likely to have effects on both sides of the net. If one player is affected for the better, the other is affected for the worse.

I think it possible to be even more specific about how this turn of events occurs. He thought he had regained his form when I deliberately made three errors. I knew he hadn't, but he could now view his earlier performance as exceptional. He therefore started playing more deliberately, taking his time, and waiting for me to make the errors. He thus gained consistency. I, on the other hand, had now to think: Perhaps his beginning performance was exceptional, perhaps he can be more consistent. Whereas I could recall noting earlier that his backhand was not very powerful, now I was thinking that although it lacked power, he wasn't making very many errors from that side. By the same process by which my appearing to grow worse initially gave him the incentive to get better, now his getting better invited me to grow worse. I began worrying about his backhand and, lest it outlast my own, started rushing and making more errors.

Illustrative of the change in thought processes is one point I remember very well. I had hit the ball hard and deep to his backhand and followed my shot to the net. He reached it but was not properly set and returned the ball high over the middle. I realized, after netting the overhead, that there was a good chance his shot would have sailed over the baseline by five feet. I had stumbled onto the Fundamental Law of Self-Prophetic Tennis. It's a lot easier not to do stupid things when you're confident that you haven't been doing stupid things. Which is why confidence and "unconfidence" tend to grow. The less confident you get, the stupider the things you do, and the less confident you get.

The temptation to go for that shot was irresistible. After all, it's a relatively easy shot, I've pushed him into a corner, I can now take advantage of it. But clearly there is no benefit to hitting a ball that is on its way out. The chance to seize an immediate opportunity, however, was so great that I couldn't help but take it. We're all much more patient when we're in control, much more in control when we're confident. We're not as likely to think, "This is my only opportunity," and therefore don't need to jump at every apparent chance.

As with many other kinds of differences, those on the

court get exaggerated. The player who is ahead is making fewer mistakes, and this makes it more difficult for the opponent to believe that he's even made one (and thus he hits the "out" ball prematurely.) The player who is behind is making more mistakes, and this makes him bend over backward not to make another (and thus he doesn't volley the ball that falls well inside the baseline). We hit it when it's out, don't hit it when it's in, and come to realize that it's only those ahead who get the "breaks."

The fact that in tennis there are numerous opportunities for decisions, for smart choices as well as stupid ones, affords more opportunity for the exaggerating effects of self-fulfilling prophecies to take hold. And this is another reason why we witness such phenomena as "momentum" and "confidence," such results of each thinking he is more or less in control, he has gained or lost his "edge," the opponent is much better or worse than he thought. There are shots that not only can be hit in various directions and with various speeds but, as the last example illustrated, can be taken or not taken. The more you've proven yourself smart in the past, the more likely you are to do so in the future.

But the definitions of past and future are variable, and this allows changes in "momentum" to occur. The Austin-Evert match described in Chapter 6 illustrates how the effects of being smart last until one is outsmarted, and how one would do well, if she senses that she has been outsmarted, to create a situation that will regain what she has lost.

In baseball, for example, one wouldn't expect so much to hinge on what one thought of himself. The game is slower, the teams change only every eight minutes or so, and thus one terrific catch will not so easily translate into a home run. But in tennis, recall that a mistake of one side is an immediate point for the other, that shots follow one another with great rapidity, and that doing well on one side of the court means accomplishing something both offensively and defensively. Therefore, doing well has more opportunity to build on having done well, good offense and defense are closely connected, and what is a trend for one player is a corresponding, but different, trend for the other. There is a greater influence on what's about to happen as a function of what one thinks is about to happen as a result of what *has* happened.

Some might argue that if our self-image is so critical, we should, perhaps, be able to work on it directly. Why isn't pretending we already *are* better all we have to do to *get* better?

Indeed, this is the psychopathic solution. Most of us are not so easily duped. Because we know we're pretending. Because we need something else, namely a sign from the world out there—the opponent's missing or our making good shots—that we're better. Just pretending we received an "A+" on the test doesn't fool us. Only the one completely divorced from reality can succeed with that approach.

In fact, were it not for the temptation to believe that anything that has such a mental component can easily be worked on mentally, there would probably be much greater attention to how important confidence, expectations, and self-fulfilling prophecies are. Somehow the belief exists that anything that seems so readily susceptible to mental gymnastics and yet can't be manipulated at will must be all wrong. The point is that it is not so easily susceptible to such gymnastics if we are the ones doing the manipulating. Self-deception is not so easy after all.

It therefore does no good to believe that you have beaten an opponent when you never have, although such a strategy would be indicated by this discussion of confidence. You could, however, try the following technique: Be prepared with a fixed strategy of performance, designed beforehand, if you start to lose. It sounds contrary to "changing your game when you're losing," but it's not. For by "fixed," I don't mean something you have been doing, but something you planned to do before you got out there on the court, just in case you had to. I will provide an example and explain the reasoning behind it.

When I kept getting close to an opponent I had never defeated, I realized that on many of the occasions when I almost won I had played steady points, only to be slowly weakened, moved around the court, and ultimately forced too far from the play. The temptation was to hit away on the next opportunity—the return of his next serve, for example—but yielding was masochistic. It was an easy way to end the torture for myself, since I wasn't particularly strong off the return of serve and he was quite a good server. So I adopted this strategy: I would try to make the point on the fourth shot of the rally. That is, I would go for the winner not immediately, but off his volley or approach shot, if I could get to it. The next time the opportunity arose to go ahead, I won the point with my return of serve, although on each such previous occasion, I had lost with it. I had prepared my strategy and didn't need it. But had I not prepared it, I'm convinced I wouldn't have won the point or finally defeated him.

In this entire discussion of self-fulfilling prophecies, we have seen how much of one's performance is constructed from one's self-image. A trend arises because of the success of one's belief in his superiority and his tendency to confirm that belief in subsequent play. In direct relation to that trend, we see the weaker opponent's inability to break out of the pattern and, indeed, his tendency to exaggerate the discrepancy with a trend of his own. Had I stayed within the dynamics of the situation described above, I would, I am sure, have been pushed around the court as usual. But

I gave myself an opportunity to escape by imposing something from outside, some principle whose characteristics *did not evolve* from the previous set of shots or points. It was thus independent of what had previously transpired and unrelated to the image of myself or his image of himself, each of which would have been diminishing or growing, respectively, if tied to immediate events.

One important way to break a negative, sliding pattern is to have prepared a fixed strategy beforehand in case the pattern develops. The loser in poker loses more because part of his pattern is suddenly to change strategy because of what has just happened. He thus takes unnecessary chances and loses the patience or control that the winner can afford, that prevents the winner's taking unnecessary chances, and that results in more winning. If you make a strategic decision beforehand—should I be down by twenty-five dollars, I will not stay in the hand with less than two pair, but will bluff with every sixth hand—you have a greater chance of not being affected by the flow of each card, each raise, each hope, each diminished hope, all of which, when you're losing, works to your disadvantage. The typical loser in the stock market sells at "the bottom" because he has changed his mind, transformed his initial strategy, whatever it had been. When the dynamics themselves are doing you no good, structure the dynamics. Make a plan and stick to it faithfully.

My particular strategy worked, although it didn't have to work. I never got a chance for that fourth shot, but I was removed from the immediate situation which had gotten me into trouble. On other occasions, it wouldn't have to work this way and hasn't, but I am convinced that because I was planning ahead, I was probably moving my feet more than usual on the return, not as worried about his serve as I would have been, not as potentially victimized by the flow of events.

Or, put another way, when you're losing, some strategy, even though it may be the wrong strategy, is better than no strategy. This is the Second Law of Self-Prophetic Tennis. Even the wrong answer to a clue can get you started in a crossword puzzle, when you're stymied.

Performance varies in all of us. In tennis, it varies extraordinarily much, for a variety of reasons. But the most pervasive feeling one has, when competing, centers around how good he is, how good he's appearing, how good his opponent is, who is currently favored, what chance he has of winning. When the opponents are relatively evenly matched, that feeling is potentially, if not actually, shifting all the time. One of the most satisfying of moments—and one religiously avoided by those who fear proving themselves better than another—is to win against someone who has won all the time, who is rated better, but against whom you always felt you had a chance if you could win but once. To realize in the middle of a match that such an opponent is making errors that you thought only you were capable of making, getting "tentative," responding to your winners with confusion, and seeming to ask himself if it's really possible he can lose is often the turning point of the match and of the subsequent play between you.

Is it unfair to take someone whose technical skills have always seemed superior to yours and prove yourself a winner? Only if one allowed that technique were all there were to it. But realizing that your own technique has varied with feelings of confidence is to realize that being "better" has more to it. Is it sadistic to have one's own confidence emerge in direct proportion to the opponent's dropping off of confidence? Only if one thinks it's the only alternative to being masochistic. Where do you think much of *his* confidence was coming from? Is it possible to go further, completely ignore "reality," and proceed solely on the basis of your own construction of it? Comes the revolution, and I'm sure we'll hear the choral answer from all the released manic-depressives, schizophrenics, paranoids, hysterics, hypomaniacs, psychasthenics, and other psychopaths, currently satisfying society's constructions by their interment, then turning the world and its definitions inside out.

CHAPTER 11

Dynamic Statistics

Their intensity was better than ours, but my guys are pros.[1]

Ever compare intensities? It's like comparing feelings, awareness, and orgasms. You do know when one is deeper than another, but since they rarely show up on computer print-outs, it's hard to calculate the difference.

Sports and statistics have been courting for some time. Every sports broadcaster would occasionally give credit to "our statistician" for a piece of telling news. ("Our statistician tells me this is only the twelfth time in modern baseball history that a left-hander has struck out the same four men in consecutive innings.") The "box score," providing all kinds of numbers, still represents the official obituary of the game. "Best" is always defined numerically—most victories, highest percentage; and records are established at the extremes of the numerical scale—fastest, longest, strongest.

Of late, it appears, the courtship has grown into a full-fledged romance. It wasn't always that one knew immediately how many shots on goal the Atlanta Flames had missed through the second period, or what a batter's life-

---

[1] Dick Motta, coach of the Washington Bullets basketball team, after his team had lost a game in the playoffs, quoted in *The New York Times*, May 12, 1978, A19.

time playoff average against a certain pitcher was *through the previous inning*, or—heaven help us!—the number of unforced errors Chris Evert hit off her forehand in this match compared to all other matches.

NOT EVERYTHING THAT'S COUNTABLE COUNTS

Can one be cynical about the progress that all these numbers represent? Indeed. If the intent is to learn something about important events in the game, about what might be instrumental to winning, then most of the data provided are not useful. For one thing, events that are critical sometimes appear to defy description, or at least quantification —like Motta's "intensity." As I'll show later in this chapter, such events needn't be so mysterious, but we have to learn how to become attentive to their occurrence.

A second cause for skepticism is that the purpose of most sports statistics appears to be something quite different from signaling events of importance. Not knowing what counts or how to measure what counts, and armed with the speediest computers the network can provide, statisticians calculate anything that can be quantified in the hope that something may prove significant. At the very least we'll have plenty of data to keep us interested in other matters, such as who hit, jumped, or threw the longest, highest, and fastest. At some point, for example, in box-score history, someone must have decided to keep track of "assists" in a number of sports. And the main result of that decision, it would appear, is that records of "most assists" can now be kept in baseball, basketball, and hockey. That the significance of the assist varies not only among these sports but also among events certainly goes unrecognized. If someone continually passes because he's afraid to shoot, he may be costing his team a lot more opportunities than he's providing them. Is a baseball player to be congratulated because the other team hits the ball to him? Does someone count the number of intercepted potential assists in hockey?

The harm in this practice of multiplying statistics is not merely that we waste time and effort over the insignificant, not merely that we can then use our data to prove anything (like the biorhythmicists, whom I'll discuss shortly), not merely that we lose interest in the mathematical approach to understanding, but that the statistics themselves succeed in defining the extent of our knowledge. The same consequences also apply to research in the social sciences, particularly psychology, where most of the time the experimentalist hires his statistician and plugs in the computer before he's decided what's important.

While tennis is certainly coming up with its own new statistics as it grows in popularity and feels the need to count more things, probably the best current example of a sport in search of more statistics is football. The Washington Redskins, I learned at some point last year, were the fourth best team in the National Football Conference in preventing their quarterback from being "sacked." And from that information I learned why people often feel "you can prove anything with statistics." Like awards to the ninth runner-up in Ms. Universe contests, or the fifth runner-up in six-person pin-the-tail-on-the-donkey contests, the records can support practically anyone for the title. One team allows fewest points per game, another fewest yards per game, another fewest yards rushing, another fewest yards rushing per run, another fewest percentage of passes completed against, and I'm sure that Tampa Bay will soon have its claim in for best defense, allowing, as it doubtless does, fewest field goals by a left-footed Hungarian in the first quarter (on Monday nights). And as if the sheer quantity of numbers pouring out weren't enough, it's also becoming clear that some statisticians may be working out their own primitive psychological defenses through record-keeping. How else to account for the latest football statistic around: injuries to various sections of the body correlated with position played. Informing us that the chances are five times as great that you'll have knee problems if you're a quarterback rather than a cornerback is probably as accurate as the information that you'll have five times greater a chance of having liver problems if you become a writer rather than a surgeon—and about as helpful.

Instead of a box score, I would prefer a different summary in tennis. It would consist not of how many unforced errors someone hit off the backhand or what their aces-to-double-fault ratio was, because I do not know if these events have significance, much less how much. It would consist of a number of events that are discussed throughout these chapters and that point the way to what matters—points won by risky or conservative strategies, matches lost after the opponent talks or you feel guilty, points won in streaks. But it would also consist of the following, which summarize much of what is critical:

a. After the Long Anything;
b. After the Lost Opportunity;
c. After the Return from the Brink;
d. After a Take That!

It is no accident that significant events become significant by what happens "after." The *change* they produce constitutes their importance. Sports that are dynamic, that potentially change a lot, offer much more dramatic interest than those that don't. (In cricket, it takes a week-*end* to figure out who's ahead, much less for a team to "come from behind.") Tennis, because of the way it is scored, and because offense and defense are all mixed up, is the most changeable.

THE LONG ANYTHING

The winner of a long-drawn-out point, game, or set wins more than the point, game, or set. The reasons for this were mentioned in Chapter 2. It is psychologically more devastating to come close to winning and then not to win than to be out of it from the start. It is not so easy to dismiss the occasion as unlike you, or your effort as halfhearted, when it has been close. If it was prolonged, you were obviously trying. If it was long, you had many opportunities to win it that are now lost.

There is, in tennis, some acknowledgment of this principle, but not nearly enough. We could keep better track. The most difficult occasion to keep track of would be the long point, because that is not summarized in any collection of data, but it is not impossible. All you need do is count the number of times the ball goes over the net, and predict beneficial results for the winner of an extremely long rally. It is easier to keep track of long games—although still difficult, because game scores are also not given in the typical, summarizing data. Only by accident, if we happen to be watching or if it gets reported in the body of a news article, do we learn that the game went to five deuces. The easiest one to keep track of is the long set, defined as one that takes the maximum or near the maximum number of games. The prediction would be that the long set would be followed by the winner's having a relatively easy time of it afterward.

Any look at scores from matches supports the last point. Vilas takes the third set, 7–6, against Connors in the 1977 U.S. Open, and wins the match with a fourth-set victory, 6–0. (In the finals of the same tournament the year before, coincidentally enough, Connors won the third-set tie-breaker against Borg, and went on to win the match with a fourth-set victory.) In the women's final of the same tournament, it's Evert over Turnbull, 7–6, 6–2. In the French Open, 1978, it's Barazzutti over Dibbs in the quarter-finals, 6–2, 7–6, 6–1. The score was particularly appropriate to the hypothesis, since the tie-breaker in the second set went to 11–9—a long, *long* set—producing, afterward, a significant margin of victory. In the Washington Star International, 1978, Connors defeats Higueras in one semifinal, 7–6, 6–2, and Dibbs wins over Orantes in the other, 7–5, 6–0. A look at the scores in *The New York Times*,[2] on a random day, in a random tournament, reveals: Dalton over Anlio, 7–6, 6–2; Smith over Casabianca, 7–5, 6–2; in the juniors, it's Lendl over Venter, 6–4, 6–1. The only exception to this pattern is Goolagong over Evers, 6–1, 6–3— and those scores, since the first set hadn't been close, constitute less of an exception than a different pattern.

I am not suggesting that a contrary pattern—for example, 6–4, 7–6—never occurs, but that proper statistics will reveal how little it occurs relative to the pattern predicted after "The Long Anything." As they do, the psychological explanation will gain further support.

As an example of the long game, we have one reported by United Press International: [3] "The 64-minute match [between Evert and King] needed ten minutes to decide the first game, a duel that went to deuce five times. Mrs. King, 34, fought off two break points, but on the third, she missed a drop shot, and Miss Evert was on her way. . . ." Evert won the set, 6–0, and on a drop shot, no less—an occasion potentially critical, because it announces, when you miss, that you've been outsmarted.

As an example of the long point's having serious effects, I can cite my own recent experience. I was in a very close first set with someone I had beaten regularly until the previous time we played, when he had won for the first

---

[2] *The New York Times,* December 25, 1977, V3.
[3] *The New York Times,* March 27, 1978, C3.

time. The stage was set for reasserting control or seeing the tide change. It reached 4–4, with every game having gone to deuce at least once. In the ninth game, we played an extremely long point, the ball going over the net at least a hundred times, it appeared. I knew while playing it that this point would be decisive. And I think he knew too, because after we'd hit about twenty shots in the rally, both of us played very conservatively, not wanting to err. This tactic, in fact, prolonged the rally. It was probably the most excruciating point I ever played, since I knew it was important and knew it would be foolish to take a chance. The temptation to "hit out"—either to get it over with or to win finally—was considerable, especially in view of the actual physical fatigue that grows during a long point if you're not one of those who runs sixteen miles a day. Eventually, I won because my opponent couldn't resist any longer. He came in on a ball of medium depth, hit the approach shot hard, and netted it. I went on to win 6–4, 6–0.

LOST OPPORTUNITIES

'Tis better never to have come close than to have come close and lost—"better," as signified by what happens subsequently. We can see this operating on a number of levels. When you're close to winning a match, a set, a game, or a point, and then fail, the effects are severe.

By "close" to winning a match, I don't simply mean having match point. Not everyone who fails to convert his first match point goes on to lose the match. There are too many other considerations. If you're ahead, two sets to love, 5 games to 1, and 40–15, it can safely be predicted that most of the time you will win, even if you don't win the next point. The opportunity that was lost wasn't so important, since it's evident you'll have another immediately, and probably quite a few after that.

But what happens if you have a two-set lead, perhaps even with a considerable game lead, as in the above example, and then lose the opportunity by not winning in the third or fourth set. The prediction would be that you would lose in the fifth. A look at the first-round Wimbledon results for 1978 reveals the following: Tanner defeated El Shafei, 8–9, 1–6, 6–2, 9–7, 6–2; Drysdale (Robin) defeated Hrebec, 2–6, 2–6, 6–4, 6–3, 6–2; Noah defeated Ycaza, 8–9, 3–6, 6–2, 6–1, 10–8; and Hewitt defeated Handle, 3–6, 5–7, 6–4, 6–3, 6–2. In no instance of a five-set match did the winner of the first two sets win the fifth. If you can't win when it's easy, how will you win when it's hard?

When you fail to win a set that was in your grasp, the result is often similar. Probably the most famous example of this was the 1975 U.S. Open, when Orantes came back to beat Vilas in five sets after being down two sets to one, and 5–0 in the third. (It's also another example of a set sequence like the one described above.)

Close encounters of the third kind—naturally—are most important. They consist of the failure to win a game that you feel you should have won. The best example is the 40–0 lead that vanishes. In the Laver-Gerulaitis match discussed in Chapter 2, Gerulaitis, ahead 5–4 and 40–0, had three set points (and match points). He lost the lead, then the game, then the set (and match) in a tie-breaker. In the Evert-King semifinal Wimbledon match of 1978 (described in Chapter 1 as being so "psychological"), King served at 40–0 for 3-all in the third set. She lost the lead, made only two points for the rest of the match, and lost 6–2 in the third.

Systematic records of the effects of "the return from 0–40" are impossible to collect from the published reports of matches, since the data do not contain the point-by-point score. You have to be watching. But if you are, you will discover one of the most emphatic events of tennis. Some further examples should suffice to confirm its importance.

The Connors-Rosewall match described in Chapter 3 began in this interesting fashion. Connors got to 40-all on Rosewall's serve in the first game, and then broke his serve on the next point (they were playing "no ad" scoring). In the next game, Rosewall had a chance to get right back as he went ahead 0–40 on Connors' serve. Connors won the next four points and the game. Here are the subsequent happenings: Connors won the set, 6–0, and the match, 6–0, 6–2. After the "sudden death" point in the second game, Connors won the next six points in a row, and 15 of the next 17. (Important statistics, nowhere kept.) And in the third game, the one immediately following that missed opportunity by Rosewall, Connors won at love with these four points:

a. Rosewall errs on a groundstroke;
b. Rosewall rushes the net on his serve
   and volleys out;
c. Rosewall misses *completely* a ground stroke
   with his (famous) backhand;
d. Rosewall double-faults.

Egregious errors for anyone, and not likely to have been caused by nothing. (I don't think I've ever seen that "whiff" —at 0–30—on a ground stroke in a professional match, except when the player was completely out of position.)

A simple statistic would have told an important story. Rosewall had won 60 percent of the points in the first two games, up to the point when Connors turned the tide. He won a total of 20 percent after the second game. To keep such statistics, however, you have to know what to be looking for.

In the Tanner-Connors match described in Chapter 2, the one in which Tanner had a new "image," Connors, serving for the first time in the second game, came back from 0–40. Tanner was promptly broken in the next game, and Connors was never behind after that. A 2–0 lead for Tanner, bolstered by the image of resurrection, could have produced something quite different. It is interesting to note that the opportunity again arose, this time for Tanner, in the fifth game of that first set. Connors was ahead 0–40, then lost a point to 15–40, then smashed at the net to win the game and go on to a relatively easy victory. A very different story might have unfolded had Tanner won that statistically unimportant, obscure, and forgotten point at 15–40. One more and Connors would have Lost an Opportunity.

To keep myself in good company, I'll cite another example from my own experience. I was playing the top-ranked player on my local "ladder" for the first time and, much to both our surprise, I was doing relatively well. It was an eight-game "pro set" (the winner is the first to win eight games), and the score was 5–4, 0–40 on his serve. One more point and we'd be all even, well into the match. And three chances for my "equalizer." He came back to tie, take the game and—guess what?—the set at 8–4. I must have been wondering, "When will I get another opportunity like this one?" and for good reason. Not only did I never get that close again that day, but the scores on the only subsequent occasions we've played have been 8–1 and 8–0. The difference became exaggerated not only for the match but for our careers. This may help to explain why some players seem to maintain superiority over others of relatively equal ability. They probably played a close match at some point early in their encounters, and the loser became plagued with the Lost Opportunity syndrome.

Within a rally, the Lost Opportunity consists of the missing of an easy shot. When the "sitter" is netted or hit over the baseline, the effects are severe. "What do I need to win, if I can't win with that?" is the likely reflection. Examples are the overhead missed (although, as explained in Chapter 9, it is not as easy as it looks), the volley missed when the opponent is pulled off court, the drop shot reached and then missed, and the double-fault.

Many instances of the effect of double-faulting can be cited. In Chapter 2, some of its causes were discussed— "How terrible if I do it!"—but of even greater interest is its effect: "How terrible that I did it!" Watch not their mistakes, someone once said, but what they do after their mistakes. In the Laver-Gerulaitis match mentioned earlier, Gerulaitis, in the final-set tie-breaker, double-faulted at 5–3. Instead of having three match points, he was now even on serve. An Opportunity Lost. He then proceeded to double-fault at 5–6, on *match point*. In the Tanner-Connors match, Tanner double-faulted at 15–30 of the ninth game, then went on to be broken for the first time, and to lose the set and the match quickly. In the finals of the Washington Star International, 1978, Connors, leading Dibbs 7–5, 5–4, 15–0, served a "double." He then proceeded to lose the match game by double-faulting *twice more* in the game, and netting a volley. Dibbs, not to be outdone, "doubled" at 5–5, game point, and then immediately "doubled" again.

In the 1978 finals of the U. S. Open, Chris Evert, Ms. Consistency, double-faulted three times in one game against Pam Shriver. Borg, not usually one given to volatility either, must have been watching. In the men's final against Connors, he double-faulted three times in the first game of the match, and twice more in one game in the second set.

When the proper tennis box score is completed, it will pay close attention to one of the sport's primitive laws: Double-faults beget double-faults.[4] And the reason has nothing to do with sudden physical deterioration.

---

[4] Located one step above on the sophistication ladder is the law: Aces beget double-faults. The reason, however, is quite different. Having achieved something exceptional, one assumes the exceptional is unexceptional. The result is error. The irony is that success would have been more probable had it not occurred.

RETURNS FROM THE BRINK

Somewhere there is a tennis myth wandering about that suggests you should never be thinking about the score, that the top performers never do, that such preoccupation interferes with performance or concentration. Let me quote Bjorn Borg on the subject of "no ad, sudden death" scoring. "I think I prefer the regular scoring system. This is too sudden. You start to get nervous even when you're ahead 3–2, and serving. You think, if I lose this point, then I can lose the game on the next one. Yes, it does affect the decisions you make on how to play a point." [5] That comment should put to rest, first of all, the belief that the best are not concerned with the score. They are thinking, although all may not be as aware of it as Borg, even of the concrete consequences of losing a particular point. And secondly, Borg's remark demonstrates much more than simply that thinking of the consequences makes you nervous. It suggests that confidence, in "normal" scoring, builds with the knowledge that losing a particular point will not put you in a "sudden death" situation. And it further suggests that the knowledge of having come back from the verge of defeat cannot help but add to one's performance.

In all the situations described as Lost Opportunities, therefore, the opponent should gain by having Returned from the Brink. And does. Each illustrates that the eleventh-hour rescue results, statistically, in improved performance for one side. There are three major reasons for this, each mentioned earlier as distinctive to tennis:

a. Offense and defense shift rapidly. This adds to the significance of having come back from the brink on a particular shot. When you hit a winner off your opponent's missed opportunity, you have reclaimed the offense from

[5] *The New York Times*, March 27, 1978, C3.

the most defensive of positions. Thus, the added importance of the passing shot you hit when he doesn't put away the easy volley or the overhead. When you throw the man out at home with a perfect peg of four hundred feet, you're still on the field. In tennis, you're always "up." And while basketball, hockey, and football have somewhat more rapidly switching offenses and defenses than baseball, you still have to go the "other way" when you block the shot or the field goal attempt. The intercepted pass which is run back for a touchdown or results in an easy lay-up for the other team or gives the hockey team a "breakaway" is highly significant, but it is the exception in these other sports rather than the rule as in tennis.

b. Closely allied to the first distinction is that you score immediately in tennis when the opponent loses his opportunity on a rally and you return from the brink. In effect, the point counts *double*. When you hold the other team at the one-foot line, you don't score seven points. In tennis, when you withstand the best of the opposition, you don't have to do your own scoring in addition. The loser of the opportunity can't rely on his defense to hold you off when you come the other way.

c. Because the scoring system is arranged into units and sub-units, there are potentially many more significant brinks. The biggest deficit in a game is 0–40 and, as we've seen, it is not only possible to come back from but it is highly significant when one does. You can't be ahead more than two sets to love. Blocking a lay-up when you're losing by 30 points in the last quarter will rarely turn the game around.

TAKE THAT!

We are, after all, despite our fancy neuroses and our proclivities to masochism, quite primitive beings. We tend to react strongly to our own or others' overt demonstrations of power. The final critical occasions I want to consider are those shots that show physical or mental power. The best two examples are the successful overhead and drop shot.

Missing the overhead was earlier found to be important. But so is making it. (The overhead, one might say, is therefore important.) The overhead represents success punctuated, quite literally, with power. It is unreturnable when successful. It often bestows an air of confidence upon the smasher and seems to diminish his opponent. Notice the winner's strut and glare after he hits it, and the loser's inability to look back for a time. But notice too that there is often a string of subsequent points for the smasher.

In the finals of the U.S. National Indoor Championship, 1978, Tim Gullikson was holding his own against Connors until Connors smashed an overhead. The match was close up to that point, but then Connors coasted home. He finished the game quickly and immediately broke Gullikson's serve in the next. In the match cited earlier, Evert and Austin struggle, and the tide turns whenever each is successful with her overhead.

Tennis allows us to be smart as well as strong; indeed, showing you're smart is a sign of strength. The drop shot, when it works, announces "I've outsmarted you." The biggest reason why it is rarely recommended by tennis sages is probably because it is risky both ways. Fail with it, and you've been outsmarted. But make it, and there are dividends. I watched two completely different sets on my local courts when a player who had failed with a drop shot early in the first made one early in the second. 6–1, nondrop-shotter, in the first; 6–0, drop-shotter, in the second. In that Evert-Austin match just mentioned, the only events interrupting the ebbing caused by overheads was the flowing caused by drop shots.

Although it now may not seem that way, not all events are critical. Collecting more data on the particular occurrences described, especially events subsequent to them, will help confirm what is. There is, of course, a risk. We might actually learn a few things. And with that knowledge, some of the mysteries will vanish. Will our hero command such admiration when it becomes known that he played the right odds by coming to the net? Will sport be as much fun when we understand what's going on? Will life be as human and dramatic and romantic and spontaneous when we can say, with greater accuracy, who's about to double-fault? Figuring things out, trying to make accurate predictions, and even psychology itself are often resisted because of the danger not so much in missing the mark as in hitting it.

AN EXCEPTION: THE OPPOSITE OF A GREAT TRUTH IS ANOTHER GREAT TRUTH[6]

Which sounds like the ultimate cop-out, but it's not. Avoiding a couple of critical exceptions would be, for they're not really exceptions—they just appear to be. Sometimes the loser of a close set goes on to win the next handily. And sometimes an obvious display of stupidity or impotence works to one's advantage.

An example of the first type occurred when I was playing a much younger and more stylish opponent for the first time. The first set went to 6-all, without a service break (the only time I can recall such a professional rhythm to any match I've played) and I won the tie-breaker by two points. He won the second set, 6–0, and the match, 6–7, 6–0, 6–4.

What happened? I thought I was supposed to coast home in the second set. Was I so exhausted by the close

---

[6] Adapted from "The opposite of a great truth is also true," attributed to Bohr by W. McGuire in "The Yin and Yang of Progress in Social Psychology: Seven Koan," *Journal of Personality and Social Psychology*, *26*, 1973, p. 455.

encounter that I had nothing left? I doubt that fatigue explains anything. We did, after all, go on to play a close third set. As I reflected on the turn of events, I recalled that my opponent did come out immediately in the second set and start hitting powerfully, apt testimony to the conventional wisdom of "changing one's game when losing." He rushed the net on each of my relatively short shots, smashed a couple of volleys, and won the first game at love. And I'm convinced that those first few points of the second set had a decided psychological effect on each of us.

When the loser of the close set does something different for the first few points and it works, a highly critical time is reached. Both players now have an occasion to reevaluate their worth in terms of the hotly contested first encounter and this new turn of events. Rather than think, I gave my best, now what can I do? the loser can easily say, All I had to do was rush the net a couple of times and the whole thing would have been different. Rather than conclude, I can take his best shot, the winner by a narrow margin may say, Uh-oh, he's caught on to what to do. I had to wonder, after those first few points, whether I hadn't been lucky in the first set that my opponent hadn't played the game he should have. This thought was made more likely by his apparent classic form. An entirely different meaning thus enveloped the match, and I'm quite sure that had he missed one or two of those volleys early in the second set, the usual expectation would have been fulfilled. I might have won it as decisively as he did.

A famous example of the second type—an obvious blunder—occurred in the Evert-Navratilova finals at Wimbledon in 1978. Navratilova, in the middle of the second set, missed an overhead completely. This seemed to turn the match around in her favor. She herself reported that it woke her up, and she went on to win the match and dethrone Evert in the third set.

The missed overhead that results in collapse does not really apply in this instance, since Evert had been well ahead up to this point. Had Navratilova been winning, it would have been interesting to see whether the embarrassing miss turned the match against her. But it certainly seems like an exception, and is worth trying to explain.

I missed seeing that particular event, but I would bet that Navratilova did things very differently on the next few points. There is no way to tell, of course, from any of the records, but changing something may have constituted what she meant by having been startled out of her slumber. Perhaps she became more aggressive, instead of playing back. And perhaps it worked for her on those first few points. If so, the incident would be very much like the one described above. The critical event serves as the impetus for a significant change in strategy which, if it works immediately, turns the match the other way.

There may be yet another, more psychological reason for the turn of events. A poor performance often embarrasses the opponent. She may identify with it and, knowing that it's atypical, seek to help the other overcome its effects. When Evert later reported, after having lost, that Navratilova may have wanted to win more than she, was she recognizing in herself some sensibility that prevented her from taking advantage of her opponent's embarrassingly poor shot? If so, she may have unconsciously changed her own game to her disadvantage. No statistic will tell us all that, but attention at the right time to the right events can at least inform us whether she too did things differently.

Having analyzed the only outstanding exception to the incidents of importance dealt with in this chapter, let me take the finals of that same tournament and report on the events as I saw them, and as doubtless will be recorded and reported after the Psychodynamic Revolution.

WIMBLEDON, 1978

It was a rare treat. Borg and Connors in the men's finals; Navratilova and Evert in the women's. The acknowledged world's best, the Number 1 and 2 seeds, in both matches. And all on television. Some of the (hidden) highlights:

1. Before the men's match, it had been predicted by one of the telecasters that Connors would win in a short match (three or four sets) and Borg in a long one (five sets). No explanation was given. Borg won, 6–2, 6–2, 6–3 and no comment was made about the prediction. The extrovert-introvert accounts for the result. Having fallen behind at the beginning, Connors couldn't come back.

2. Borg was broken in the second game of the match, putting Connors ahead, 2–0. At 15-all in the third, Connors tries a drop volley. Borg reaches it and puts it away. Connors has been Outsmarted. This is a potential Turning Point. Connors then double-faults at 15–30, loses the game, and does not win another game in the set.

3. The fifth game of the first set goes to a number of deuces. Connors loses it, the last point being a very short ball that he reaches but doesn't put away. Borg reaches it and passes him. A Lost Opportunity. Connors loses the next three games and the set.

4. In the sixth game, at 2–4, deuce, Connors tries a drop shot which again Borg reaches and uses to pass him. Outsmarted. Connors loses the game and set.

5. On the last point of the first set, Borg serving at 5–2, 40–30, Connors errs on a short approach shot. Another Lost Opportunity. Connors loses the set and the match in straight sets.

6. At 1–1, deuce, in the third game of the second set, Connors again Misses an Opportunity, an approach shot.

He misses another one to lose the game, and his decline is further accelerated.

7. With Borg serving at 2–1, 0–40, in the second set, Connors has a chance to get the break back with one of the next three points. He Loses the Opportunity; Borg Returns from the Brink, and goes on to win handily.

8. Connors is staying even in the third set. At 3–3, 15–0, he double-faults. An Easy Shot Missed. He doesn't win another game.

9. Connors never consistently rushed the net. True, Borg passes well. But not coming to the net often enough was how Connors had lost in big matches to Orantes and Vilas. Borg too must have been pleased when he stopped coming.

In the first two sets of the women's final, between Evert and Navratilova, there were many examples of the tide shifting with critical points. I'll concentrate on a few significant events in the third and decisive set.

1. In the first game, Evert is serving at 15–0. Navratilova gets an easy overhead at the net, which she puts away, and adds a little Take That! stare. Evert goes on to lose the game at 15, the set, and the match.

2. In the second game, the umpire changes a linesman's call when Navratilova stares at him. He does this without even asking the linesman if he was sure of his call. Evert seems to have clearly thought Navratilova's shot was out, that the linesman was correct. But all are feeling guilty because earlier Narvatilova had called an Evert shot "in" that was called "out" by the linesman, and they had replayed it. This was the critical 30–0 point, which, if won by Evert, would have been significant. She is denied the Opportunity, by guilt, of reducing the significant two-point lead.

3. At 4–2, Evert, having just gained a break in the sixth game, misses an easy approach shot after Navratilova has hit a poor, shallow shot. A Lost Opportunity. Instead of holding serve to take a 5–2 lead, Evert gets broken at 15 and loses both her advantage and eventually the match.

4. At 5–5 and serving, Evert misses another approach shot. She misses still another on the very next point, and loses the match 2–6, 6–4, 7–5.

There appears to be more to this game than bending, stretching, and getting the racquet back.

BIORHYTHMS: IT'S A BAD THEORY, BUT IT DOESN'T WORK IN PRACTICE

To summarize: most statistics are meaningless. The importance of noting critical incidents such as the ones described is to provide more relevant information. Simply counting unforced errors, for example, because you're interested in tennis performance is like counting the number of dreams a person reports if you're interested in imagination. Before counting, you'd want to know what the relationship was or if there was one at all. Who knows? Maybe errors are a good sign. Show me a man who makes no errors and I'll show you one who doesn't take enough chances.

But better no theory than bad theory. The best example of statistics gone wrong are "biorhythms," currently enjoying some popularity. You name it, they'll prove it. The winner of any event will be explained on the basis of individual rhythmic patterns. It is such a good example of what not to do with numbers that it is worth considering in some detail.

Patterns are derived simply from the individual's birth date, a la astrology, but because the length of the three cycles—emotional, physical, and intellectual—varies, figuring out your chart requires the help of an accountant (or an *idiot savant* who can tell you in two seconds that April 28, 1573, was a Wednesday).

Like the astrological chartists, the ESP chartists, and the UFO chartists, the biorhythmic chartists offer us a vision that is immensely appealing. A way of understanding beyond ourselves, despite ourselves. No will power, attention, or memory necessary, since there are no failures for which we're accountable. All is fixed at birth. In the words of one of their less verbose gurus, What is is.

Begging his pardon, What is often ain't. From ancient Heraclitus, who depicted the ultimate content of the world as impermanent and in a state of flux, through Immanuel Kant, who established the impossibility of demonstrating a world of existence apart from our apprehension of it, to Gestalt Psychologists, who emphasized the dynamic, relational aspects of things, to some two hundred scientists who found it necessary to deplore publicly the popularity and theoretical gobbledygook of astrology and its fellow pseudo-sciences, it should be apparent that reality is not so simple that all we need do is surrender ourselves to it.

As with all such attempts to explain performance with a single set of arbitrary principles, it is not their failure to account satisfactorily for events that confirms suspicion, but their success. All things, from the beginning of the universe to Walter Paton's gaining over 200 yards rushing against the Minnesota Vikings. All things, from Jimmy Carter's election to Uri Geller's psychokinesis to your feeling blue at seven A.M. on Monday morning.

More specifically, all truth to the biorhythmicists is *after* the fact. Want to know why Moseley missed three field goals or Jim Marshall ran the wrong way with the football? They'll tell you. Since it happened already. Statistically, that just won't do. Especially when there are not only those three dimensions that are vital, but all kinds of points on those dimensions and countless combinations. For example, there's not only a high and low for each cycle, there's a critical time, when one trend is shifting to another. So even "highs" aren't all they're cracked up to be, since—it turns out after the fact—some do better at lows or during critical periods.

Anyone with a little training in mathematics, or an ear for pundits' explaining the hour-by-hour movement of the stock market, or some experience with double Venuses rising in your Sagittarius can predict where this kind of analysis goes. The number of potentially critical occasions begins to exceed the number of days in your life. Or, if the critical period in changing from low to high is more critical than the high period itself, we then have a right to ask whether things are looking up when they're not looking down, or when they're not looking down as much as they were yesterday.

—"Jack, we're getting rich."

—"We're making money, finally?"

—"No, we're losing."

—"But we're losing less than last year?"

—"No, but the increase from last year's losses to this year's losses is less than the increase from those of two years ago to last year's. The rate at which our losses have increased has slowed."

(And if that's increasing, the rate at which the rate of increase is going up has slowed.)

Next year we'll be millionaires.

By the biorhythmic accounting, everything is potentially critical. And when you add—critical for whom? Player, spouse, coach, opponent?—it is not at all surprising that every event can seem to dance to the sound of a biorhythmic drum.

If there is some support for their principles, it lies in the discussion (Chapter 10) of self-fulfilling prophecies. If players are told prior to the big game that they're invincible, they may well prove to be. And if I can read a month ahead of time that Vilas will be at an intellectual "conflict point" in his WCT match with Borg, I suspect Vilas can too. There's nothing quite like being primed for conflict for producing it.

While none of us as yet can explain performance with unerring accuracy, it certainly is eminently more reasonable to base our theories and search for confirming evidence on what makes scientific or psychological sense. That effort may well fail here, but not because our ups and downs have been correlated with planetary, muscular, or fluid movements at our moment of conception.

CRISIS INTERVENTION

If the biorhythmicist's conception of "critical" were accurate, there would be nothing to do but participate or stay home. Those alternatives contrast sharply with the policies that follow from "critical" incidents as described in this chapter. There are some simple things to do, in the manner of intervening, other than simply avoiding the issue. (Some of these have been described in other chapters, particularly Chapter 6.)

Alertness to the potentially devastating incident is a beginning. If your opponent has missed an easy shot, do not press him. He is likely to miss some more, to rush when he shouldn't. When Rosewall made those four bad mistakes in the match with Connors, he wasn't being pressured at all by his opponent. Connors had only to relax and not try for winners to capitalize on the opportunity. The principle is simple:

1. *Do not pressure your opponent after he's lost an opportunity.*

Many of us do just the opposite. We charge, with renewed vigor and confidence, following the point gained by the opponent's double-fault or his missed overhead. This gives him a chance to get back his confidence. If lying back and taking advantage of his downfall seems too cruel, remember that the true masochist shares that feeling. It should not have to be added at this point that maximizing your opportunities is not equivalent to taking unfair advantage of your opponent. Only through his not playing perfectly do you have a chance to win.

2. *Do not pressure yourself when you've lost the opportunity.*

Again, we tend to do the opposite. Following our missed overhead, we get back quickly for the next point, so that everyone will forget the last. Resist the temptation to try to erase the error immediately. In fact, take extra time. You can't undo it. Connors does this repeatedly, after his mistakes, so much so that opponents sometimes get annoyed at his deliberation. But he is well within his rights to take the extra second or bounce the ball another time, especially when the opponent is so eager to rush right in.

3. *If you've won a long set, be alert to the opponent's changing something on the very next point. If he does, and succeeds on more than one point, then you change something too.*

If you win the first few points following the tie-breaker, do nothing exceptional. But if you don't, do. Had I been alert to my younger and fitter opponent's rushing out in that second set described earlier, I could have changed my own style a bit, before it was too late. Even if he was a better net-rusher than I—which he was—had I done it once or twice, he would not have been as successful as to change things around so dramatically. At the very least, the awareness of the possibility that he would change tactics would have prevented my being so affected by it.

4. *If you've lost the long set, change something immediately.*

It follows from the above. When you've lost the tie-breaker, the opponent's confidence will be very high, and without a sudden change on your part, he is likely to prove more patient. It's the familiar, "Change a losing game."

5. *If you're ahead comfortably, try avoiding critical occasions.*

Don't create brinks from which your opponent can return. There are enough already there. If you can avoid it, don't lob or drop-shot when you're ahead.

6. *If you're losing steadily, try to create a critical occasion.*

This also follows from the above and was mentioned in Chapter 6. The important thing is to recognize that you're doing it when you're doing it. Many a potential turn in the match has been prevented not because the player on the way down has done the wrong thing, but because he thinks he has. Lob. Drop-shot. When they're not necessary, they often don't work, but if you recognize that likelihood before you do it, you won't exaggerate the effects by throwing up your hands and feeling nothing's possible. Do them again. Or you may not have to.

And when all else fails, hit for the fences until you're down 0–40, and then try to come back.

Epilogue: No Apology

It sometimes appears that those who would analyze this and other games must do so apologetically. Among many, particularly in these liberated days, winning is held in very bad repute. Or, rather, the intention to win. It's all right to do all right, as long as you don't appear to have that objective. Once you've made it apparent that you'd really like to win at something, you're a representative of the aggressive, combative male ego which, feeling so insecure, must constantly conquer to bolster itself. As an example of this view, I would cite a recent analysis of "The Super Bowl Ritual." [1] The author equates the event with a "masculinity match," one that is similarly present in the excesses of male chauvinism and nationalism, particularly patriotism and going to war.

A second commonly heard view is that winning itself is not such a bad thing, but rather the inevitable tendency to become totally committed to it. Who hasn't heard the famous line, attributed to Vince Lombardi, "Winning's not everything, it's the only thing"? Now, such opponents of competition say, is that how we want to bring up our kids?

I emphatically believe that both views are mistakes. Winning is not a primal sign of aggression that we sophisticates

---

[1] W. Farrell. "Super Bowl Ritual: Mix Masculinity with Patriotism," *The New York Times*, January 15, 1978, V2.

on the evolutionary scale must stamp out (aggressively, no doubt), nor is it permissible only as long as it doesn't become a habit. For both positions tend to identify the result, "winning," with the process, "winning," and thereby conveniently ignore an important distinction. (For the grammarians, it is notable that any ". . . ing" word is both a gerund and a participle, and thus can refer either to a product [How do you feel about *winning* the Open?—that is, about having emerged the victor], or a process [Hooray, we're winning—that is, we're ahead.]) It is not the nature of having won that gives "winning" a bad name, but rather how often the event takes place through offensive means.

There are, no doubt, terribly offensive competitors—types who are so self-absorbed that they jump at every opportunity to point out their strengths and your weaknesses. Who rub your nose into the ground when they've won, or stick out their tongue at you in humiliation. Who endlessly bemoan and make excuses for their losses. Who will do anything to win.

But there are terribly offensive "noncompetitors" also—the kind who say, "Hey, take it easy, it's only a game," or "Don't get so excited," or "I didn't mean anything by it,"—who, much more insidiously, attempt to belittle your effort at integrating your actions and your feelings. To identify wanting to win with humiliating others is to equate everyone in the football audience with supporters of the half-time rituals of flag-waving and drum rolls. It is no more accurate to interpret competitive spirit as a "macho" tendency than it once was to interpret its absence as a signal of the "sissy."

Even as I type in the decorous confines of the Allen Room of the New York Public Library, I sense the compelling push of other keyboards. As one starts, a syncopated rhythm often begins—sometimes harmonious, sometimes discordant. Will competition produce the best book? I'm not sure, but certainly I'm confident that it is not in the way, that it is pushing me to work, to join, and to be interested in others and their interests. Psychologists even have a name for it—"social facilitation." In how many undetected places is the desire to excel another form of the urge to win? Can one really become the best poet one can, or the cleverest raconteur, or the most insightful at a seminar or on the shrink's couch with no eye or ear sensitive to the reaction of others, the audience? Is the desire to be good, even at social work, not competitive?

I think the guilt attendant on many who would win if they tried, but who refrain for fear of identification with the humiliating, aggressive types, severely limits their expressive opportunities. It's a relic of a distaste for Vince Lombardi's alleged ethic, or a wish not to be identified with a leering Ilie Nastase, cursing his opponents when he's losing, or an effort not to become the kid who starts cheating at every opportunity once he realizes that there are shortcuts to becoming a winner.

Yet, distinguishing wishes that originate in hero-worship from those that more truly express a person's needs is often psychology's purpose. So, similarly, is the importance of supporting those wishes that are representative of a person's ideals, despite their being shared with unpleasant company. Even on a tennis court, one can live well.

Index

Perfectionism, 29, 31–34, 36–37
Perry, Fred, 165n
Personality (as branch of psychology), 20, 121–22, 125, 129. *See also* Freud, Sigmund, and Freudian theory; Jung, Carl
Personalization, 41
Philadelphia 76ers, 76
Pittsburgh Steelers, 162, 163–64
Points. *See also* Scoring
critical, 21, 24, 111, 196–212
and risk-taking, 167–72
Poker, 40, 155, 165, 190
Pressure, 34, 93, 97, 174, 175, 215–16. *See also* "Choking"
Professors, 26, 92, 130–31, 155
Psychoanalysis. *See* Freud, Sigmund, and Freudian theory
Psychology. *See also* specific branches
limitations of, 8–9, 43, 91, 140–41, 195, 207
as opposed to technique, 7–8, 31, 79, 177, 191, 203, 212
popular misconception of, 51
potential of, 9–10, 18–20, 129, 141, 169, 206, 215, 220

Psychopathology, 19, 176–77, 188, 191–92

Quietness of tennis, 24, 25, 68–69, 74. *See also* Concentration

Rallying
and guilt, 56–58, 74, 84–86, 88
and playing games, 21, 24, 103–5, 131–32, 133, 144
on schedule, 138
Ralston, Dennis, 34
Ramirez, Raul, 8, 113–14
Rank, Otto, 112
Rational therapy. *See* RET
Refereeing, 20, 21–22, 24–25, 29, 54, 63–64, 65, 68–69, 73, 74, 79, 86–88, 105, 116–17, 211
Reid, Kerry Melville, 68–69
RET, 31, 43, 77, 78, 81
Risk and caution, 20, 23, 25, 29, 37, 99, 154–55, 160–75, 184, 185–86. *See also* Gambling
Risky-shift phenomenon, 158–60
Riverside Drive, 52
Role-playing, 104
Rosewall, Ken, 71–73, 179, 201, 215

Scoring, 21, 93, 94, 106, 168, 196, 204–5. *See also* Points
Self-image, 61, 178, 188, 189

Unforced errors, 100, 171, 194, 196, 212
U.S. Open
  1975, 35, 128, 200
  1976, 197
  1977, 68–69, 117, 118, 181–84, 197
  1978, 203
Urban tennis. *See* Adjacent courts; Assertion; Spectators

Vilas, Guillermo, 22–23, 117–19, 166, 179, 182–84, 197, 200, 211
Volleying, 38, 57, 58, 85, 167

Warm-up. *See* Rallying
Washington Bullets, 76, 193n

Washington Redskins, 17, 195
Wimbledon
  1975, 127–28
  1976, 61
  1977, 117
  1978, 17–18, 62, 200, 208–12
Wind, 23, 108
"Winner-Take-All" match, 128
Women and men, 78–79, 124, 148, 150–51. *See also* Aggression; Assertion
World Team Tennis, 24, 166
Writers, 42, 43, 196

Yerkes-Dodson curve, 77, 78
Young, Jimmy, 118